Miracle-G

Perennials

Brighten your yard with beautiful perennials

Meredith® Books

Des Moines, Iowa

Miracle-Gro Basics – Perennials
Writer: Megan McConnell Hughes
Editor: Marilyn Rogers
Contributing Designer: Studio G Design
Copy Chief: Terri Fredrickson
Publishing Operations Manager: Karen Schirm
Senior Editor, Asset and Information Manager: Phillip Morgan
Edit and Design Production Coordinator: Mary Lee Gavin
Editorial Assistant: Kathleen Stevens
Book Production Managers: Pam Kvitne, Marjorie J. Schenkelberg, Rick von Holdt, Mark Weaver
Contributing Copy Editor: Sarah Oliver Watson
Contributing Proofreaders: Stephanie Petersen
Contributing Photographers: David Cavaganaro: 22TR, 48CR, 48BR, 56TR; Alan & Linda
   Detrick: 74CR; John Glover, cover BL; Hermann Gröne: 40BR; Sunniva Harte/Garden Picture
   Library: 56BR; Saxon Holt: 44BR, 58TR, 72BR, 76CR; Rosemary Kautzky: 46T, 46B, 62TR,
   80C; Andrew Lawson: 38TR, 38CR, 68CR, 76L; Becky Long/North Creek Nurseries: 46L;
   Marilynn McAra: 74BR; Clive Nichols: 26TR, 76TR; Jerry Pavia: 22BR, 26CR, 28TR, 44TR,
   44CR, 46CR, 58BR, 72TR, 72CR, 74TR, 76BR; The Scotts Company: 12C; Richard Shiell:
   28CR, 30TR, 52CR, 66TR, 68TR, 70CR; Albert Squillace/Positive Images: 80TR; Mark
   Turner: 62CR
Contributing Photo Researcher: Susan Ferguson
Contributing Photo Stylist: Diane Witosky
Indexer: Elizabeth T. Parson
Special thanks to: Mary Irene Swartz

Meredith® Books
Executive Director, Editorial: Gregory H. Kayko
Executive Director, Design: Matt Strelecki
Managing Editor: Amy Tincher-Durik
Executive Editor/Group Manager: Benjamin W. Allen
Senior Associate Design Director: Ken Carlson
Marketing Product Manager: Isaac Petersen

Publisher and Editor in Chief: James D. Blume
Editorial Director: Linda Raglan Cunningham
Executive Director, New Business Development: Todd M. Davis
Executive Director, Sales: Ken Zagor
Director, Operations: George A. Susral
Director, Production: Douglas M. Johnston
Director, Marketing: Amy Nichols
Business Director: Jim Leonard

Vice President and General Manager: Douglas J. Guendel

Meredith Publishing Group
President: Jack Griffin
Executive Vice President: Bob Mate

Meredith Corporation
Chairman and Chief Executive Officer: William T. Kerr
President and Chief Operating Officer: Stephen M. Lacy

In Memoriam: E.T. Meredith III (1933-2003)

All of us at Meredith® Books are dedicated to providing you with information and ideas to
enhance your home and garden. We welcome your comments and suggestions. Write to us at:
Meredith Books, Garden Editorial Department, 1716 Locust St., Des Moines, IA 50309-3023.

If you would like more information on other Miracle-Gro products, call 800/225-2883 or visit us
at: www.miraclegro.com

Note to the Readers: Due to differing conditions, tools, and individual skills, Meredith
Corporation assumes no responsibility for any damages, injuries suffered, or losses incurred as a
result of following the information published in this book. Before beginning any project, review the
instructions carefully, and if any doubts or questions remain, consult local experts or authorities.

Perennial Pleasures

Perennials are prized for a trait that is rare in the world of gardening—they are predictable. Rising from the ground in spring, they unfurl lovely foliage and lengthen their stems. When the conditions are right, they send up long-lasting blooms. When winter arrives, they take a siesta before beginning the process again the following spring.

Simple soil preparation and a bit of regular care keep perennials in top form. Unlike their cousins, the annuals, perennials demand a minimal amount of weekly upkeep in order to bloom with gusto.

Plant perennials alongside small shrubs for a splash of floral interest that lasts year after year. Combine them with annuals for easy-to-grow, come-again color. Or create an entire blooming border of perennials, showcasing plants that flower from early spring until fall.

< 3 >

HOW TO USE THIS BOOK
Plant Selection Guide

Turn to the Plant Selection Guide beginning on page 21 to learn details about growing more than 30 different perennial plants. Each plant summary includes recommended cultivars and step-by-step growing tips.

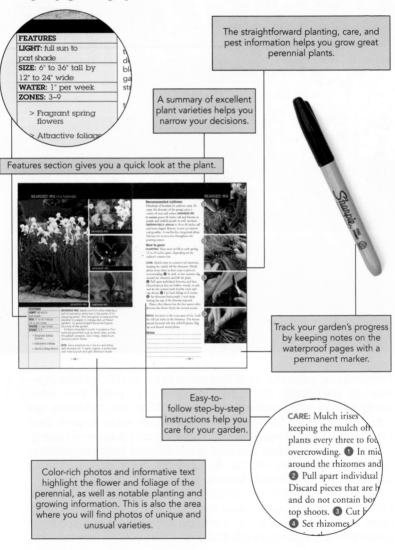

FEATURES

LIGHT: full sun to part shade	
SIZE: 6" to 36" tall by 12" to 24" wide	
WATER: 1" per week	
ZONES: 3–9	

> Fragrant spring flowers

> Attractive foliage

The straightforward planting, care, and pest information helps you grow great perennial plants.

A summary of excellent plant varieties helps you narrow your decisions.

Features section gives you a quick look at the plant.

Track your garden's progress by keeping notes on the waterproof pages with a permanent marker.

Easy-to-follow step-by-step instructions help you care for your garden.

Color-rich photos and informative text highlight the flower and foliage of the perennial, as well as notable planting and growing information. This is also the area where you will find photos of unique and unusual varieties.

CARE: Mulch irises keeping the mulch off plants every three to fo overcrowding. ❶ In mi around the rhizomes and ❷ Pull apart individual Discard pieces that are h and do not contain bo top shoots. ❸ Cut b ❹ Set rhizomes

< 4 >

Soil Preparation

Perennials need only a few key elements to grow, stay healthy, and look their best: good, friable soil; occasional watering; and a ready supply of nutrients that fuel growth and blooming. Set your perennials on a path to success by making the garden soil the best that it can be. With minimal preparation, even marginal sites can become excellent places to grow perennials.

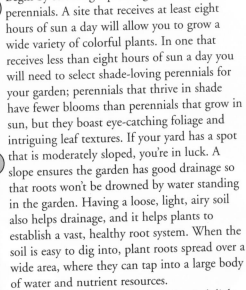

Begin by selecting a planting site for your perennials. A site that receives at least eight hours of sun a day will allow you to grow a wide variety of colorful plants. In one that receives less than eight hours of sun a day you will need to select shade-loving perennials for your garden; perennials that thrive in shade have fewer blooms than perennials that grow in sun, but they boast eye-catching foliage and intriguing leaf textures. If your yard has a spot that is moderately sloped, you're in luck. A slope ensures the garden has good drainage so that roots won't be drowned by water standing in the garden. Having a loose, light, airy soil also helps drainage, and it helps plants to establish a vast, healthy root system. When the soil is easy to dig into, plant roots spread over a wide area, where they can tap into a large body of water and nutrient resources.

If the soil in your chosen location isn't light and airy, you can loosen it in a few easy steps. ❶ Using a garden hose and flour, outline the shape of the bed. ❷ Remove sod with the help of a sharp spade or, if the garden is large, consider renting a sod cutter from your local hardware store to get the job done.

Begin preparing the soil by loosening it. Perennials grow best in 18-inch-deep beds of loose soil, but you need only dig deep enough to break up the compacted layer.

The best time to do this job is fall. You can work soil any time that it's not frozen, but doing so in fall allows time for the soil-enhancing

< 6 >

activity of worms, frost, and rain to supplement your work. Working the soil in fall also gives the amendments the time to make their changes and the soil to settle so it is ready for planting. Whatever time of year that you prepare the soil, make sure the soil is friable, or crumbles easily. To test, squeeze a handful, then open your hand. The soil should crumble readily when poked. You can loosen soil by hand or with a tiller.

BY HAND: Use a spade or spading fork to cut, lift, or reset soil. Working the soil by hand is best in small areas that have minimal compaction. Loosen the soil by inserting the fork to its full depth, then pulling back on the handle to lever the tines.

3 TILLING: Tilling is practical if the garden is large and free of perennial weeds, such as quackgrass, and tree roots. Avoid overtilling or working in wet soil. Soil broken up too many times by a tiller becomes structureless, like sifted flour. Tilling wet soil will create clods that bake in the sun and become hard to break apart.

4 Help keep the soil loose over time by spreading a 2- to 3-inch layer of Miracle-Gro Garden Soil or compost over the soil bed. Use the tiller to mix the native soil with the Miracle-Gro Garden Soil or compost.

< 7 >

Planting Perennials

You can plant perennials any time of the year, but they make the strongest start when the air is cool and the soil warm and moist. The best times to plant are midspring and early autumn, before leaves fall. Overcast and drizzly days are ideal for planting. Avoid the middle of a hot, sunny day—when water from leaves is lost more quickly than it can be replaced.

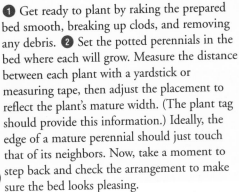

1 Get ready to plant by raking the prepared bed smooth, breaking up clods, and removing any debris. **2** Set the potted perennials in the bed where each will grow. Measure the distance between each plant with a yardstick or measuring tape, then adjust the placement to reflect the plant's mature width. (The plant tag should provide this information.) Ideally, the edge of a mature perennial should just touch that of its neighbors. Now, take a moment to step back and check the arrangement to make sure the bed looks pleasing.

For each perennial, dig a hole that is one and a half times as wide as the root ball but only as deep. Many perennials will die if planted too deeply. Take care to not plant too high either. This allows the exposed "shoulders" of the roots to dry out and prevents roots from spreading in the garden. **3** Check the depth of the hole by setting the plant in it, then laying a shovel handle or yardstick across the hole. The top of the plant's root ball should be even with the handle. Once the plants are at the right depth, backfill around them.

Water, mulch, label

4 Water each plant, then spread a 1- to 2-inch-deep blanket of bark mulch, such as Scotts Nature Scapes Mulch, over the garden. Take care to not cover the crowns and stems of plants; this encourages rot. Finally, label plants so that you remember which is which until you become familiar with your new perennials.

< 8 >

A weekly 1- to 2-inch rain shower provides most perennials with all the water they require. When Mother Nature falls short, it is up to you to supply the water. The type of soil and specific plant needs determine how much water you should actually provide. Learn about the specific water needs of common perennials in the Plant Selection Guide, starting on page 21.

Watering how-to

When watering perennials, the goal is to moisten the soil as a 1- to 2-inch rain does, soaking the ground several inches below the surface. To learn how long your sprinkler will need to run to apply an inch of water, set several straight-sided containers, such as soup cans, in the garden. Turn on the sprinkler and let it run until the cans collect an inch of water. Depending on water pressure, sprinkler type, size of the area, wind, and evaporation rate, it might take from one to six hours.

Early morning is the best time to water. At first light, the air is calm, reducing evaporation. Plus, foliage dries quickly, thwarting leaf diseases that thrive on damp leaves and high humidity. There is one exception to morning irrigation: In hot regions where water is scarce, nighttime irrigation is preferred to reduce evaporation.

Watering methods

❶ Hand-watering is adequate for newly planted or very small perennials. For larger plants, overhead and direct-to-soil watering are more efficient ways to deliver the large amount of water your plants require.

❷ Overhead systems, such as rotary and oscillating sprinklers, are good for covering large areas and rinsing off foliage. Their output is easily measured, but plants in the spray path have an increased risk of leaf diseases, and runoff on windy or hilly sites can be a problem.

< 10 >

To avoid leaf diseases, water early in the morning so plants dry quickly, reducing the chance that disease will take hold.

❸ Direct-to-soil watering conserves moisture and keeps foliage dry by applying water directly to the soil surface through a drip system or soaker hose.

Drip systems and soaker hoses can take several hours to deliver an inch of water, and it's difficult to determine when they have adequately moistened the soil. To test whether they have run long enough, dig a 4-inch-deep hole about 1 foot away from an emitter or hose and feel the soil at the bottom. If the soil feels cool and moist, the bed has received enough water.

Save Water

- Spread a 2- to 3-inch layer of mulch around plants to prevent evaporation.

- Deliver water directly to plant roots with drip lines or soaker hoses.

- In extremely hot, dry regions, water at night to cut down on evaporation.

- Select plants that thrive in dry soils such as butterfly weed, yarrow, and blanket flower.

< 11 >

Feeding

Just as you can't rely solely on rainfall for the best perennial show, you can't expect nature to supply all the nutrients perennials require. Gardeners' standards are higher than nature's. Weeding, deadheading, cutting flowers, and removing plant debris disrupt the natural recycling of nutrients. For best blooms and healthy foliage, you're going to have to feed your plants.

Plant food provides essential elements that actively growing perennials require, like the vitamins humans need to build strong bodies. The simplest method for feeding your perennials is to use a complete plant food—one that contains full a spectrum of plant nutrients. Flowering plants require about the same nutrients as other plants, with one exception: If some flowering plants are given too much nitrogen, they will grow leaves at the expense of flowers. Select a plant food formulated for flowers, such as Miracle-Gro Bloom Booster Flower Food.

Applying plant food

Perennials need the most food when they are actively growing. The best time to feed perennials is from their first growth in spring until their flower buds develop. How often you feed perennials depends on the type of plant food you use.

Most plant foods sold for home use have directions on the package. The simplest and surest way to apply them is to follow package directions.

Types of plant food

Because the nutrients in all complete plant foods for flowering plants are basically the same, the main difference lies in their convenience. Different formulations are made to be applied in different ways; the right plant food for you depends on how you prefer to work. Some of your options:

< 12 >

❶ DRY PLANT FOODS come as granules or pellets. Generally, you sprinkle them over the ground, then scratch them into the soil. Apply dry plant foods every month or so.

❷ LIQUID PLANT FOODS, such as Miracle-Gro Water Soluble All Purpose Plant Food, are concentrated powders or liquids made to be mixed with water, then sprayed onto roots or leaves every 7 to 14 days.

❸ CONTROLLED-RELEASE PLANT FOODS release nutrients over long periods of time. Osmocote Smart Release Plant Food and Miracle-Gro Shake 'n Feed are examples. They come in different forms: tablets to drop into holes, spikes to press or drive into the soil, and pellets or granules to stir into the soil. Apply controlled-release plant foods once or twice during the growing season.

< 13 >

Perennial Care

Regular perennial plant care—deadheading, cutting back, staking, and dividing—helps perennials look fresher, bloom longer, stand straighter, and grow at a healthy pace. Following the tips below, spend a few minutes a week caring for your perennials. The plants will reward you with bushels of blooms and healthy foliage.

DEADHEADING Remove flowers as they fade but before seeds begin to ripen. This stimulates the plant to develop more flower buds and bloom again. Some spent blossoms, such as those of daylilies, snap off easily. Ones atop soft perennial stems can be pinched off with your fingers. ❶ Those on thick or sturdy stems need to be cut off with a pair of pruners.

Remove individual flowers on a spike or in a cluster as they fade. Once it begins looking ratty, cut the entire flower stalk back to a side shoot or all the way to the ground. ❷ An easy way to deadhead perennials with many tiny blooms is to shear them with grass clippers.

In some instances you might not want to deadhead—when a plant has attractive seedpods, for example, or when the seeds attract songbirds to your garden.

CUTTING BACK ❸ Remove much or all of a plant's foliage to stimulate a new flush of leaves or flowers. Cutting back is a shock to the perennial, so take care. Spare newly planted or stressed perennials. See the plant descriptions in the Plant Selection Guide, page 21, for how-to information on cutting back specific perennials.

Cutting back is done most often to perennials that grow quickly, bloom before

< 14 >

summer's heat, or tend to cease growing once seeds begin to ripen. Perennials that benefit from cutting back are usually trimmed after their blooms fade. To cut back a perennial, use sharp pruners to trim all stems on the plant to within 6 inches of the soil. Water the plant regularly after cutting back to stimulate healthy new growth.

STAKING Help tall plants and those with floppy stems or heavy flowers, such as foxgloves, delphinium, and peony, stand tall. Perennials growing in soil that is too lean or too rich can get lanky and weak-stemmed, and are even more likely to need staking to stand up to their own weight and the wind. It may take a season's experience with a plant to learn whether a perennial will need staking or will stand on its own.

Stake plants in spring while they are short. The objects you use for staking might look awkward when first placed in the garden, but perennials grow so quickly from midspring to early summer that they will rapidly cloak the stakes with foliage.

Good plant stakes allow plants to move. Motion is necessary for plant growth. Grow-through supports are excellent for bushy perennials, such as globe thistle or peonies. You can use ❹ commercial grid supports or ❺ twiggy branches left over from pruning shrubs. ❻ Single stakes are best for single-stemmed perennials such as foxgloves and delphiniums. Secure the stems to the stakes with several pieces of soft twine or fabric. Begin tying the stem to the stake when it is 6 inches tall and continue every two weeks or so.

continued on page 16>>

< 15 >

DIVIDING As perennials grow over the years, they tend to spread out, crowd their neighbors, and develop dead centers in the clump. Dividing helps them maintain their health and vigor, plus you will also gain several new plants to share with friends or expand your garden.

Some perennials benefit from frequent division; bee balm, for example, is a vigorous grower and can be divided annually. Other perennials, such as peonies, rarely need divided. Consult the Plant Selection Guide, page 21, to learn more about the requirements of specific plants.

Divide perennials in spring or fall. Follow this simple three-step process.

❶ Using a sharp spade, cut around the perimeter of the perennial, angling the blade toward the center of the plant. Carefully lift the plant out of the ground. ❷ Use the spade, a hand trowel, or a sharp knife to separate the plant into sections. Each division should have three or more stems or growing points and adequate roots to support the foliage. ❸ Space the divisions according to their mature size and replant. Water deeply.

MULCHING ❹ Keep weeds at bay and reduce water evaporation with a layer of mulch. Mulch also prevents rapid heating or cooling of the soil, thereby allowing steady root growth. If an organic material is used as mulch, its particles become soil-enriching humus as they decompose.

Many materials can be used as mulch. Some of the best materials include compost, shredded leaves, cocoa hulls, and shredded bark. Spread a 2-inch layer of mulch around the plant's root zone, taking care not to let it touch the stems. The constant moisture of the mulch can rot plants. Spread fresh mulch as needed to maintain a 2-inch layer.

< 16 >

4

Care Calendar

SPRING
- Cut off and discard any foliage or flowers that overwintered in the garden.
- Divide crowded plants and replant.
- Stake tall perennials and those with heavy flowers.
- Mulch as needed.

SUMMER
- Deadhead plants as soon as flowers fade.
- Cut back fading foliage of spring-flowering perennials.
- Mulch as needed.

FALL
- Divide crowded perennials and replant.
- Cut back perennials after the first frost or when foliage withers.
- Mulch as needed.

Problem Solving

Most perennials are low-maintenance plants with few insect or disease problems, especially if the plants are well-sited and well-tended. But exceptions to the rule abound, as with all plants.

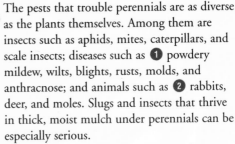

The pests that trouble perennials are as diverse as the plants themselves. Among them are insects such as aphids, mites, caterpillars, and scale insects; diseases such as ❶ powdery mildew, wilts, blights, rusts, molds, and anthracnose; and animals such as ❷ rabbits, deer, and moles. Slugs and insects that thrive in thick, moist mulch under perennials can be especially serious.

Early identification keeps your garden healthy. Regularly visit your perennials and check on how they are growing. Watch for discolored foliage, distorted growth, and plants that are growing more slowly or less densely than their neighbors.

Some pest problems, such as ❸ leaf miners, are mainly cosmetic—unsightly but not serious. You can let such problems run their course. Other pests are life-threatening; they kill plants, and you should deal with them decisively and quickly.

❹ Determining when to spray pesticides and when it's best to handpick insects or control by other means takes time and education. Learn which pests can be problems for your perennials, the type and extent of damage that's possible, the point at which natural controls quit working, and methods available for managing the pests. To learn more about pests and pest control, purchase a copy of Ortho's *Home Gardener's Problem Solver* or Miracle-Gro's *Encyclopedia of Plant Care*.

< 18 >

Prevent Pest Trouble

Healthy plants regularly fend off pests of all sorts without showing distress. Follow these tips for maintaining a pest-free perennial planting.

• Plant disease-resistant cultivars. Breeding advancements translate to a variety of plants that resist troublesome diseases. Read plant tags to learn whether the perennial is disease resistant.
• Water and feed plants regularly to maintain a strong defense system. Plants that are stressed by lack of water or nutrients let down their guard and are more vulnerable to pest attack.
• Clean up dead or diseased foliage as soon as possible to prevent the spread of disease.

Troubleshooting

Symptom	Cause	Solution
Holes in leaves or sections of leaves and flowers missing	Leaf- and flower-chewing insects such as beetles, leaf miners, and caterpillars	When damage is noticeable, spray plants with Ortho Rose and Flower Insect Killer. Plan to fend off an attack next year. Note the date when you first noticed the damage, then subtract two to three weeks. That's when to start checking the plants for damage.
Holes carved out of the middle of a leaf. Plants with this type of damage are usually in a shaded area.	Slugs or snails	Use Ortho Bug-Geta Snail & Slug Killer; at night handpick and destroy slugs and snails; use only a 1-inch layer of mulch or do not mulch at all to eliminate slug and snail habitats.
Fuzzy or white coating on leaves	Powdery or downy mildew	Spray plants with Ortho Garden Disease Control. Remove diseased leaves and debris around infected plants; water only in the morning; select mildew-resistant varieties.
Rotted black or brown sections at the base of stems or on roots	Root and crown rot	Dig up plants that show signs of root or crown rot; discard heavily infected plants. For those with less rot, cut out the diseased portions. Prevent rot by letting the soil dry out between waterings. Also, make sure plants have the correct amount of light.
Stems and foliage neatly snipped off at ground level	Rabbits	Fence whole beds or cage plants individually with ½-inch mesh wire. Fences need to be at least 18 to 24 inches tall. Repellents such as distasteful sprays or scented items may be temporarily effective.
Nibbled and trampled foliage and flowers	Deer, elk, or moose	Keep out grazers with 8-foot tall fencing. Dark plastic mesh fencing is effective and reasonably priced.

< 20 >

Plant Selection Guide

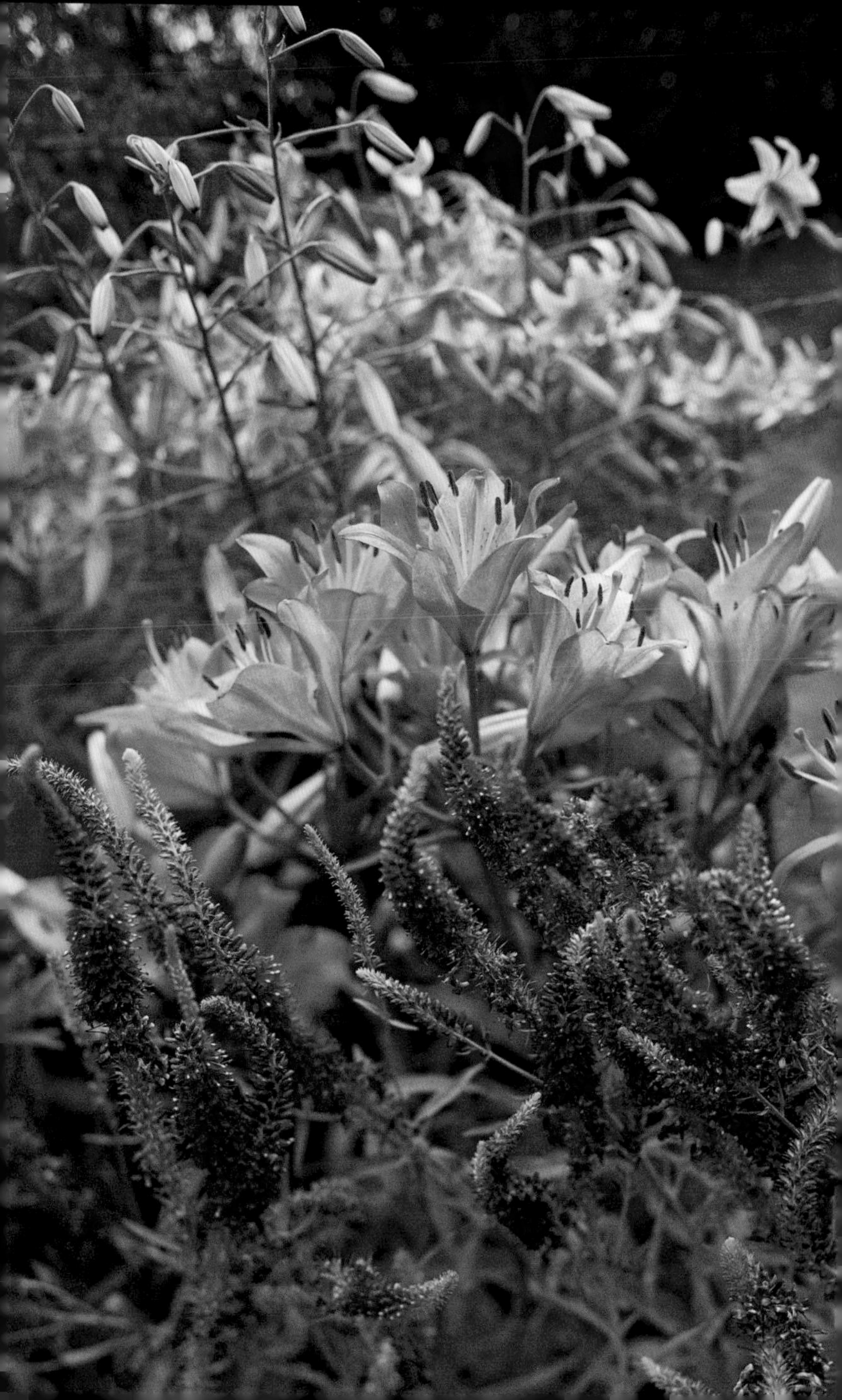

'FANAL'

'SNOWDRIFT'

HYBRID AND CHINESE ASTILBES 'PUMILA'

FEATURES	
LIGHT:	partial to full shade
SIZE:	18" to 48" tall by 24" wide
WATER:	1" to 2" per week
ZONES:	4–8

> Thrives in shade

> Long-blooming

> Prefers moist, well-drained soil

ASTILBE has dense white, red, or pink flower plumes that rise like sparklers in the shade garden. It grows in a neat clump at a moderate rate. Its finely cut, dark green foliage forms an excellent backdrop for other perennials. Good planting companions include hosta, lungwort, and coral bells.

SITE: Grow astilbe in part to full shade and moist, well-drained soil. Plants will fail in soil that dries out in the summer. Amend the soil so that it is neither too sandy nor too heavy with clay.

< 22 >

Recommended cultivars

'AMETHYST' grows to 36 inches tall and 24 inches wide and has lilac-pink blooms in early summer. 'BRESSINGHAM BEAUTY' is 36 inches tall and 24 inches wide, with bright pink blooms in midsummer. 'FANAL' (white) and 'SNOWDRIFT' (red) are early bloomers.

CHINESE ASTILBE (*A. chinensis*) grows to 24 inches tall and wide with pink blooms in late summer. It is one astilbe that grows in sun or shade and is drought tolerant. The variety *davidii* has appealing bronze-tinged leaves, bears purplish-pink blooms, and grows to 6 inches tall and 24 inches wide. 'PUMILA' blooms in pink.

How to grow

PLANTING: Plant astilbe 18 to 24 inches apart in spring or fall. Apply a slow-release plant food such as Miracle-Gro Shake 'n Feed Continuous Release All Purpose Plant Food at planting or begin using water-soluble plant food, such as Miracle-Gro Water Soluble All Purpose, three weeks after planting in spring. Cease feeding astilbe six to eight weeks before the first frost date.

CARE: ❶ Astilbe's most critical need is water. Leaves become crispy when soil is allowed to dry too much, and plants are more susceptible to spider mites. Water deeply whenever the soil begins to dry.

Spread a 3-inch layer of mulch around plants to keep soil moist and reduce weeds. Divide plants every three to four years in spring. Deadhead by cutting the flower stalks at their base. Early-blooming varieties may rebloom. Cut back plants to ground level in late fall or before new growth begins in early spring.

PESTS: Meet astilbe's water needs, and it's relatively pest-free.

Notes

_____

_____

_____

_____

< 23 >

BEARDED IRIS

JAPANESE IRIS

SIBERIAN IRIS

BEARDED IRIS

FEATURES	
LIGHT: full sun to part shade	
SIZE: 6" to 36" tall by 12" to 24" wide	
WATER: 1" per week	
ZONES: 3–9	

> Fragrant spring flowers

> Attractive foliage

> Good cutting flower

BEARDED IRIS stands out from other irises by a tuft of colored or white hair in the center of its drooping petals. This late-spring or early-summer bloomer is a staple in cottage and cut-flower gardens. Its sword-shaped leaves lend good structure to the garden.

Combine bearded iris with mounded or fine-textured perennials such as dwarf aster, yarrow, threadleaf coreopsis, false indigo, delphinium, and pincushion flower.

SITE: Grow bearded iris in full sun and fertile, well-drained soil. In warm regions, it grows best with morning sun and light afternoon shade.

< 24 >

Recommended cultivars

Hundreds of bearded iris cultivars exist. To enjoy the diversity of the group, grow a variety of sizes and colors. JAPANESE IRIS (*I. ensata*) grows 36 inches tall and blooms in purple and reddish-purple in early summer. SIBERIAN IRIS (*I. sibirica*) is 18 to 48 inches tall and bears elegant flowers. Leaves are narrow and grasslike. A trouble-free, long-lived plant, Siberian iris is attractive throughout the growing season.

How to grow

PLANTING: Plant irises in fall or early spring 12 to 24 inches apart, depending on the cultivar's mature size.

CARE: Mulch irises to conserve soil moisture, keeping the mulch off the rhizomes. Divide plants every three to four years to prevent overcrowding. ❶ In mid- to late summer dig around the rhizomes and lift the plant. ❷ Pull apart individual rhizomes and fans. Discard pieces that are hollow, woody, or soft and do not contain both healthy roots and top shoots. ❸ Cut back foliage to 6 inches. ❹ Set rhizomes horizontally 1 inch deep, leaving the top of the rhizome exposed.

Plants often bloom less the first season after division but flower freely the second season.

PESTS: Iris borer is the worst pest of iris. Look for tell-tale holes in the rhizomes. The borers spread bacterial wilt that will kill plants. Dig up and discard rotted plants.

Notes

_____
_____
_____
_____
_____

< 25 >

BEE BALM *(Monarda didyma)*

'GARDENVIEW SCARLET'

'MARSHALL'S DELIGHT'

BEE BALM

'PETITE DELIGHT'

FEATURES	
LIGHT: part shade to full sun	
SIZE: 36" tall by 24" wide	
WATER: 1" to 2" per week	
ZONES: 4–9	

> Attracts bees and hummingbirds

> Long-blooming

> Also known as Oswego tea

A North America native, **BEE BALM** is easy to grow and prized for its long bloom period. Its fringed flowers appear in lilac, pink, red, and white. Bee balm does well in containers or borders and is a favorite nectar source for bees and butterflies. Pair it with ornamental grasses, daylilies, perennial salvia, black-eyed Susan, or iris.

SITE: Choose a site that is in full sun or that receives light afternoon shade. One that has good air circulation is a must to avoid powdery mildew. A moderately fertile, well-drained soil is best.

< 26 >

Recommended cultivars

Cultivars with resistance to powdery mildew include 'AQUARIUS', pink flowers and bronze foliage; 'BOWMAN', purple flowers; 'GARDENVIEW SCARLET', large bright red flowers; 'MARSHALL'S DELIGHT', pink flowers; and 'VIOLET QUEEN', violet-purple flowers. 'PETITE DELIGHT' is also mildew-resistant. It has pink flowers and is 12 to 18 inches tall.

How to grow

PLANTING: Plant bee balm 18 to 24 inches apart in spring or autumn; apply a slow-release plant food at planting. Keep the soil uniformly moist.

CARE: Bee balm usually requires no staking; but where they do, circular grow-through supports do a good job of keeping plants upright. Deadhead to encourage reblooming. Trim plants back in fall once frost withers the foliage.

Bee balm can spread rampantly; plan to divide it every two or three years to keep the size of the clump under control.

Divide plants in spring or in fall. ❶ Cut back stems to 3 to 4 inches above ground level. Dig around the plant, then lift the entire plant out of the ground. ❷ Plunge a sharp spade through the roots. ❸ Plant pieces with healthy roots and shoots and toss the others.

PESTS: Bee balm is susceptible to powdery mildew. To reduce its occurrence, select mildew-resistant cultivars; choose sites with good air circulation; keep soil moist, not soggy or bone dry; and avoid overcrowding.

Notes

_____

_____

_____

_____

_____

< 27 >

'GOLDSTURM' BLACK-EYED SUSAN

'AUTUMN SUN'

'INDIAN SUMMER'

'PRAIRIE SUN'

FEATURES	
LIGHT: full to partial sun	
SIZE: 30" tall by 42" wide	
WATER: drought tolerant	
ZONES: 3–8	

> Low maintenance

> Blooms from midsummer to frost

> Attracts birds and butterflies

From midsummer to frost, **BLACK-EYED SUSAN** unfurls hundreds of dark-centered, golden yellow daisies. This clump-forming, low-maintenance perennial's coarse texture and mounded shape combines well with finer textured and upright plants. Good partners include blazing star, false indigo, delphinium, globe thistle, Joe-Pye weed, ornamental grasses, and speedwell.

SITE: Grow black-eyed Susan in full or part sun and moist, humus-rich soil. It will tolerate wet and poorly drained soil, wind, salt, and heat.

< 28 >

Recommended cultivars

'GOLDSTURM' is a lovely compact plant with long-lasting flowers. 'VIETTE'S LITTLE SUZY' is just 12 to 15 inches tall and wide. 'AUTUMN SUN' (also called 'Herbstsonne') grows 5 feet tall and has drooping lemon-yellow blooms with green cones. 'PRAIRIE SUN' has a striking green center. 'INDIAN SUMMER' grows 3 feet tall with large flowers.

GIANT CONEFLOWER *(R. maxima)* has large blue-green leaves and small yellow flowers with prominent narrow cones. It grows 4 to 8 feet tall and 2 to 3 feet wide. Zones 5 to 9.

How to grow

PLANTING: ❶ Plant black-eyed Susan 18 to 24 inches apart in spring or fall. Apply slow-release plant food at planting.

CARE: Water deeply during extended periods of drought. ❷ Deadhead plants to prolong bloom and keep them tidy. Or leave the sturdy seed stalks for winter interest. Plants will self-sow. ❸ Staking is necessary for some of the taller black-eyed Susans to ensure they stand upright. Use grow-through stakes or single stakes and string.

PESTS: Black-eyed Susan is basically pest free. Leaf spot and crown rot may develop in older, crowded clumps. Dividing plants every four to five years avoids these problems and maintains vigor, size, and quantity of bloom.

Notes

_____

_____

_____

_____

_____

_____

< **29** >

BLANKET FLOWER *(Gaillardia × grandiflora)*

BLANKET FLOWER

'BURGUNDY'

'GOBLIN'

'FANFARE'

FEATURES

LIGHT: full sun

SIZE: 36" tall by 18" wide

WATER: 1" per week

ZONES: 3–10

>Blooms all summer

>Easy to grow

>Tolerates heat and cold

BLANKET FLOWER is covered from early summer until early autumn with red and yellow daisies that have warm, red-brown centers. The flowers attract butterflies and are good in fresh cut arrangements. Plant this short-lived, loosely upright perennial near the front of a border. Blanket flower blends well with yarrow, coreopsis, and ornamental grasses.

SITE: Grow blanket flower in full sun and fertile, well-drained soil. Plants tolerate infertile soil.

< 30 >

Recommended cultivars

'BABY COLE' has 3-inch yellow-tipped bright red daisies with burgundy centers. 'BURGUNDY' has wine-red flowers. 'RED PLUME' has brick-red flowers. Those of 'TOKAJER' are dark orange, and 'GOBLIN' has deep red flowers with yellow tips. 'FANFARE' is a new cultivar with yellow, tubular flowers.

How to grow

PLANTING: Plant blanket flower 18 inches apart in spring or fall. Apply slow-release plant food at planting or begin using water-soluble plant food three weeks after planting. Cease feeding six to eight weeks before the first frost date.

CARE: Water deeply when the soil is dry. ❶ Apply 3 inches of mulch in summer to help retain soil moisture. ❷ Spent flowers are pretty messy looking. Deadhead to clean up the plant and stimulate reblooming. Plants will develop many new flower buds. ❸ Cut plants back to within 6 inches of the ground in August to promote fall bloom and new foliage growth.

Divide as necessary in spring or fall by digging around the root clump and lifting. Blanket flower overwinters better if the spent foliage remains on the plant after frost. Wait until early spring to cut back and clean it up.

PESTS: Powdery mildew, downy mildew, and rust occasionally trouble blanket flower. To avoid these diseases, water in the morning so the foliage dries quickly in the sun. Space plants at least 18 inches apart for good air circulation.

Notes

_____
_____
_____
_____
_____
_____

< 31 >

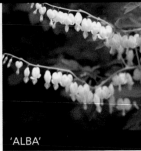

'ALBA'

'GOLD HEART'

'LUXURIANT'

OLD-FASHIONED BLEEDING HEART

FEATURES	
LIGHT: full to partial shade	
SIZE: 4' tall by 2' wide	
WATER: 1" per week in spring and early summer. Rainfall is sufficient the rest of the year.	
ZONES: 3–9	

>Heart-shaped flowers

>Blooms in spring

>Deer- and rabbit-resistant

Loved for its long, arching stems and dangling, pinkish red, heart-shaped flowers in early spring, **BLEEDING HEART** is a hardy plant for shade gardens and woodland borders. Flowers are superb in fresh cut arrangements. Plant bleeding heart with other shade lovers such as coral bells, hosta, astilbe, and foam flower.

SITE: Grow bleeding heart in full to part shade and fertile, well-drained soil that is high in organic matter.

< 32 >

Recommended cultivars

The cultivar 'ALBA' has pure white blooms. 'GOLD HEART' has pink flowers and eye-catching yellow-green foliage. FRINGED BLEEDING HEART (*D. eximia*) is a mounded plant with attractive finely cut foliage. It blooms intermittently from late spring through early autumn. 'LUXURIANT' has pink flowers and blooms almost continuously from spring until frost.

How to grow

PLANTING: Space bleeding heart 15 to 24 inches apart in spring or fall. After planting, water deeply and spread 3 inches of mulch around, but not touching, the plant.

CARE: Apply slow-release plant food at planting or begin using water-soluble plant food three weeks after planting in spring. Stop feeding after flowers develop. Bleeding heart often dies back (goes dormant) in midsummer. Interplant it with other shade lovers and astilbe to cover the empty space.

In spring or fall, divide plants every three years, or when vigor declines. Cut back foliage to 6 inches above the ground. ❶ Cut around the plant with a spade, then lift the clump out of the ground. Slice the clump into pieces with the spade or break it apart. ❷ Make sure each division contains at least five shoots and a mass of healthy roots. ❸ Dig a generous hole to accommodate the roots, plant, water, and mulch.

PESTS: Slugs and snails are occasional pests. Treat severe infestations with Ortho Bug-Geta Snail & Slug Killer. Wet soil during the summer may contribute to disease problems; let soil dry out between waterings and improve air circulation.

Notes

< 33 >

'LANCASTRIENSE'

'PATRICIA'

BLOODY CRANESBILL

'JOHNSON'S BLUE'

FEATURES

LIGHT:	full sun to partial shade
SIZE:	8" tall by 12" wide
WATER:	1" per week
ZONES:	4–8

> Attractive ground cover

> Red fall foliage in cold climates

> Flowers sporadically throughout summer

BLOODY CRANESBILL is a great low-maintenance perennial for the front of a border or a rock garden. It is also a good ground cover. Magenta-pink flowers with darker veins and white eyes appear from early summer to early autumn. The finely cut foliage is attractive. Pair bloody cranesbill with perennial salvia, foxglove, lamb's-ears, and bearded iris.

SITE: Bloody cranesbill prefers full sun or light shade and well-drained, moderately fertile soil. In hot, sunny areas, it will do best with afternoon shade.

< 34 >

Recommended cultivars

'ALBUM' has white flowers. 'ELSBETH' has pink flowers with darker veins and vibrant red leaves in autumn. 'JOHN ELSLEY' is prostrate with rose-pink flowers and deep green leaves. 'LANCASTRIENSE' has pale pink flowers and grows just 4 inches tall. 'PATRICIA' (*G. psilostemon*) is 18 to 20 inches tall with magenta flowers. 'JOHNSON'S BLUE' is a popular hybrid geranium with blue flowers.

How to grow

PLANTING: Plant bloody cranesbill 12 inches apart in spring or fall. Apply slow-release plant food at time of planting.

CARE: Water deeply when the soil is dry. Even though the plants are low-maintenance and drought tolerant, they grow and bloom best if they receive 1 inch of water a week.

Deadhead to stimulate reblooming.

❶ If plants become leggy, cut back foliage to 6 inches above the ground to promote more compact growth. Leaves are evergreen in mild climates. In cool climates they turn crimson in autumn.

Divide plants in spring or fall every two to three years to maintain vigor. Use a spade to lift the clump. ❷ Separate plants by pulling apart the root system. ❸ Reset pieces that contain healthy roots and shoots.

PESTS: Meet its cultural preferences, and bloody cranesbill is relatively pest free. Occasional diseases include downy mildew, powdery mildew, and bacterial blight. Ensure good air circulation among plants and avoid transferring diseases on your tools from one plant to another.

Notes

_____

_____

_____

_____

< 35 >

CHRYSANTHEMUM *(Chrysanthemum × grandiflorum)*

MIXED CHRYSANTHEMUMS

'MEGAN'

'MARILYN'

'YELLOW SARAH'

FEATURES

LIGHT:	full sun
SIZE:	12" to 36" tall by 12" to 24" wide
WATER:	1" to 2" per week
ZONES:	4–9

> Blooms from late summer to fall

> Many flower forms and colors

CHRYSANTHEMUMS send the growing season out in a flurry of colorful flowers. This clump-forming perennial is swathed with blooms in shades of crimson, orange, yellow, pink, cream, or purple. Complement chrysanthemums' mounding growth habit with upright companions such as purple coneflower and ornamental grasses.

SITE: Garden chrysanthemum prefers full sun and fertile, well-drained soil.

< 36 >

Recommended cultivars

Hundreds of chrysanthemum cultivars exist, blooming in a variety of shapes, sizes, and colors. If you plan to grow mums as perennials, work with the nursery staff to select a cultivar that is hardy in your area. Potted mums from florist shops are not usually perennial plants. They might overwinter in Zones 9 and 10. Treat them as annuals everywhere else.

How to grow

PLANTING: Plant mums 12 to 24 inches apart in spring or fall.

CARE: ❶ Pinch stem tips every few weeks through June to encourage compact growth. ❷ Cut foliage and spent flowers to the ground in autumn after frost withers growth; in mild locations, leave the plants erect for winter interest. ❸ Spread a 4- to 5-inch layer of straw over plants for added cold protection. Mums are short-lived perennials in Zones 4 and 5 and may be grown as annuals in cold areas. Divide plants every three years in spring to maintain their vigor.

PESTS: Viruses stunt plant growth, mottle leaves or turn them yellow, and distort the shape of leaves, sometimes puckering them. Dig up and destroy affected plants. Control the insects that spread the viruses, including leafhoppers, aphids, spider mites, and whiteflies. Spray with insecticidal soap, Ortho Systemic Insect Killer, or Ortho Rose & Flower Insect Killer.

Notes

_____
_____
_____
_____
_____
_____

< 37 >

'NORA BARLOW'

'ADELAIDE ADDISON'

CANADIAN COLUMBINE

MCKANA HYBRIDS

FEATURES	
LIGHT: full sun to partial shade	
SIZE: 30" tall by 24" wide	
WATER: will tolerate drought; will also thrive when it receives 1" to 2" of water per week	
ZONES: 3–9	

> Cottage garden favorite

> Attracts hummingbirds and butterflies

COLUMBINE'S nodding flowers appear from late spring to midsummer and sport up to 4-inch-long spurs. Blooms are often two-toned; some cultivars have double flowers. Plant columbine near the front or middle of the border where you can enjoy its blooms up close. Columbine often self sows and naturalizes well. Good companions include hosta, lady's mantle, and astilbe.

SITE: Grow columbine in full sun or partial shade and fertile or average, well-drained soil. The plants are short-lived, but they will reseed, thus replacing themselves or spreading around the garden. Hand-weed unwanted seedlings.

< 38 >

Recommended cultivars

The MCKANA HYBRIDS strain is popular for its large blooms in a variety of colors. BIEDERMEIER GROUP HYBRIDS reach 20 inches tall and 12 inches wide. Bloom colors include white, pink, purple, and blue. MRS. SCOTT-ELLIOT HYBRIDS grow 36 inches tall by 24 inches wide. Plants bloom from late spring to midsummer in a variety of shades.

How to grow

PLANTING: Plant columbine 18 to 24 inches apart in spring or fall. In hot areas grow it where it will receive some afternoon shade.

CARE: Apply slow-release plant food at planting or use a water-soluble plant food every two to three weeks. Cease feeding six to eight weeks prior to the first frost date. ❶ Deadhead spent flowers by cutting bloom stalks back to the nearest set of mature leaves to encourage reblooming. Water deeply whenever the soil is dry.

After two to three years the base of this plant will become woody and blooms and foliage will begin to decline. Replace plants when this occurs. If blooms are not harvested, plants self-seed. Cut plants to the ground in late fall after frost withers the foliage.

PESTS: Leaf miners bore tunnels through the leaves, tracing a visible trail on the leaf surface. Apply Ortho Systemic Insect Killer early in the season. Remove infested leaves.

Notes

_____

_____

_____

_____

_____

_____

_____

_____

_____

< 39 >

'BUTTERFLY BLUE'

CREAM PINCUSHION FLOWER

'PINK MIST' COMPACT PINCUSHION FLOWER

FEATURES	
LIGHT: full sun	
SIZE: 24" tall by 30" wide	
WATER: 1" per week	
ZONES: 5–8	

> Attracts butterflies

> Long-blooming flowers

> Heat tolerant

From midsummer until fall, tufted purple, pink, or white blossoms rise above **COMPACT PINCUSHION FLOWER**. In warm regions the plants will bloom on and off through winter. All pincushion flowers are heat tolerant and pest resistant. For a dramatic effect in the garden, plant them in groups of three or five. Compact pincushion flower can also be grown in containers. Good companion plants include roses, chrysanthemum, and Russian sage.

SITE: Grow compact pincushion flower in full sun and moderately fertile, well-drained soil.

< 40 >

Recommended cultivars

'BUTTERFLY BLUE' has purplish-blue flowers beginning in midsummer. 'PINK MIST' bears purplish-pink flowers. Both cultivars bloom until the first frost.

Cream pincushion flower *(S. ochroleuca)* forms a low rosette of foliage from which wiry 3- to 5-foot-long stems sprout. Plants bloom all summer in off-white.

How to grow

PLANTING: Plant pincushion flower in spring or autumn 18 to 24 inches apart.

CARE: ❶ Apply slow-release plant food in spring. Deadhead spent blooms by cutting flower stalks back to the ground to encourage reblooming. Plants lightly self-seed in the landscape. Seedlings are easy to remove by hand-pulling.

Divide plants in spring every three years to maintain their vigor. Dig around the root clump and lift the plant. Use a sharp spade to slice through the root system. Reset portions that contain healthy roots and top shoots and discard any pieces that do not. Water deeply.

Prune compact pincushion flower in fall once frost withers the foliage. In warm winter regions, enjoy occasional winter flowers and prune the plant in early spring.

PESTS: All pincushion flowers are relatively pest-free when their cultural requirements (sun, soil, planting depth, and moisture) are met.

Notes

< 41 >

'ROSE SWAN'

'MARY TODD'

'BROADWAY MAGIC'

DAYLILY

FEATURES	
LIGHT: full sun to partial shade	
SIZE: 6" to 48" tall by 12" to 36" wide	
WATER: 1" per week	
ZONES: 3–10	

> Grows well in nearly all conditions

> Showy flowers

> Many flower colors available

DAYLILIES are some of the most popular, widely planted perennials. These foolproof plants are available in a large range of sizes, flower colors, shapes, and bloom periods, and they are among the easiest perennials to grow. Combine a selection of early, mid-, and late-blooming varieties for summer-long blooms. Daylilies, with their clean and attractive foliage, blend beautifully with most perennials. Choose dwarf selections for containers. For a naturalized look plant daylilies in large drifts.

SITE: Daylilies grow best in full sun or part shade and fertile, moist, well-drained soil. They will tolerate drought and low fertility.

< 42 >

Recommended cultivars

More than 30,000 named daylily cultivars exist. A sampler: 'HYPERION' grows 48 inches tall and has fragrant rich yellow midseason flowers. 'STELLA DE ORO' is 12 inches tall and has reblooming, bright golden-yellow flowers. 'HAPPY RETURNS' is another yellow-flowered repeat bloomer.

How to grow

PLANTING: In spring or fall plant daylilies 12 to 36 inches apart, depending on their mature size.

CARE: Apply slow-release plant food at planting or begin using water-soluble plant food three weeks after planting in spring. Cease feeding four to six weeks before the first frost date. ❶ Break off spent blossoms to keep daylily plants attractive while other flowers open. Remove the entire stalk when all buds have opened. ❷ Divide plants in spring or fall every three years to control their spread. Long-established clumps can be thick and dense and may require a sharp ax to slice through them. Normally, though, you can slice the root balls with a spade or set two garden forks back-to-back into the clump, then push apart the handles to break the clump into pieces. ❸ Reset portions that contain healthy roots and top shoots.

Prune plants back after frost withers foliage. In mild areas let the foliage stand and prune it back in early spring.

PESTS: Daylily rust occasionally plagues plants. Cut back foliage of infected plants to the ground. Remove the foliage of surrounding plants to limit the spread of the disease.

Notes

_____

_____

_____

_____

< 43 >

'ASTOLAT'

'GALAHAD'

DELPHINIUM   'BLUE BIRD'

FEATURES	
LIGHT: full sun to partial shade	
SIZE: 5' to 6' tall by 2' to 3' wide	
WATER: 1" to 2" per week	
ZONES: 2–7	

> Cottage garden favorite

> Needs moist, rich soil

DELPHINIUM'S petal-packed spires are an eye-catching sight in the early summer garden. For a stellar show, plant delphiniums in groups of three. The white, purple, or pink flowers are superb cut or dried. Combine delphinium with later-blooming tall plants such as garden phlox, Joe-Pye weed, and ornamental grasses.

SITE: Grow delphinium in full sun and fertile, well-drained soil. A spot with light afternoon shade is ideal. This plant does not perform well in high-heat areas.

< 44 >

Recommended cultivars

Many cultivars exist, falling into several general groups. The **ELATUM GROUP** has large flowers on stalks up to 5 feet tall. **PACIFIC GIANT HYBRIDS** may grow as biennials or annuals and have 3- to 5-foot-tall flowers. **'ASTOLAT'**, **'GALAHAD'**, and **'BLUE BIRD'** are in this group. **CONNECTICUT YANKEE HYBRIDS** have loose stalks of flowers in early and late summer. *D. GRANDIFLORUM* has large, airy flowers and is often grown as an annual.

How to grow

PLANTING: Plant delphinium 12 to 36 inches apart in late spring or in fall. Delphiniums are heavy feeders so feed plants regularly with a water-soluble plant food. Cease feeding six to eight weeks prior to the first frost date.

CARE: Water deeply when the soil is dry and mulch plants to help conserve water. ❶ Tall cultivars require sturdy staking to stand straight. Insert a single stake beside the plant when it is young. Tie the stem to the stake with soft twine. You can also grow them against fences or walls for support. Deadhead delphinium by cutting back spent spikes to encourage small, flowering side shoots. Cut plants to the ground in autumn after frost withers the foliage.

Divide delphinium plants in early spring every three years for healthy, vigorous plants.

PESTS: Common pests include snails and slugs, powdery mildew, bacterial leaf and fungal leaf spots, Southern blight, and root rot. Apply Ortho Bug-Geta Snail & Slug Killer around plants. Ensure good air circulation or spray with Ortho RosePride Rose & Shrub Disease Control to alleviate powdery mildew. Remove and destroy rotted plants and do not replant perennials susceptible to Southern blight or root rot in the same spot. Improve soil drainage and let soil dry thoroughly between waterings.

Notes

_____

_____

_____

_____

< **45** >

FALSE INDIGO (Baptisia australis)

'PURPLE SMOKE'

WHITE WILD INDIGO

'SCREAMIN' YELLOW'

'PURPLE SMOKE' FALSE INDIGO

FEATURES	
LIGHT: full sun	
SIZE: 5' tall by 2' wide	
WATER: drought tolerant	
ZONES: 3–9	

> Purple flowers

> Impressive size makes it a valuable plant for the border

> Decorative seedpods

Count on **FALSE INDIGO** for brilliant purple flowers in late spring or early summer followed by decorative, green, pealike seedpods that eventually turn black. This shrubby perennial is useful for the back of a border, as a specimen plant, or as a low hedge. It tends to have bare ankles and pairs well with 2- to 3-foot-tall plants that cover them up, such as perennial geranium. Other good companions include black-eyed Susan and purple coneflower.

SITE: False indigo does best in full sun and well-drained soil that is preferably sandy yet nutrient-rich.

< 46 >

Recommended cultivars

'PURPLE SMOKE' has charcoal-green stems and pale lilac flowers; it grows in Zones 3 to 8. **WHITE WILD INDIGO** *(B. alba)* is a North America native plant with 12-inch-long white flower spikes. **'SCREAMIN' YELLOW'** is relatively new with bright yellow flowers.

How to grow

PLANTING: Plant false indigo 24 inches apart in spring or fall.

CARE: Apply slow-release plant food at planting or begin using water-soluble plant food three weeks after planting. Cease feeding six to eight weeks prior to the first frost date. False indigo tolerates drought but sets more flowers and forms a dense clump with regular watering. Apply 3 inches of mulch in spring to retain soil moisture and reduce weed seed germination.

❶ Deadhead to prevent reseeding, cutting just below the spent bloom. If you would like the attractive black seedpods for indoor arrangements, let the pods develop fully on the plant, then harvest.

PESTS: Plants are relatively pest-free, but powdery mildew and fungal leaf spot may occur. You can apply fungicides or learn to tolerate light infections (less than 15 percent damage to foliage). Avoiding overcrowding and improving air circulation around plants will also help control the diseases.

Notes

_____
_____
_____
_____
_____
_____
_____
_____
_____
_____

< **47** >

FOXGLOVE *(Digitalis purpurea)*

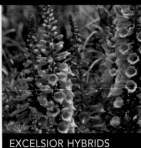

EXCELSIOR HYBRIDS

YELLOW FOXGLOVE

FOXGLOVE | STRAWBERRY FOXGLOVE

FEATURES

LIGHT: full sun to part shade	
SIZE: 3' to 6' tall by 2' wide	
WATER: 1" per week	
ZONES: 3–8	

> Cottage garden favorite

> Cutting flower

> Deer and rabbit resistant

FOXGLOVE'S 3- to 6-foot-tall spikes are cloaked with bell-shaped purple, pink, or white blossoms for three weeks or more in early summer. It is a good candidate for woodland and cottage gardens where it can self-sow at abandon. Good companions include iris, roses, lady's mantle, and lilies.

SITE: Foxglove grows in full sun or part shade and fertile, well-drained soil. In warm regions, it does best when planted where it will receive afternoon shade. Foxglove is a heavy feeder. Improve sandy or clay soil by incorporating a 3-inch layer of compost before planting.

< 48 >

Recommended cultivars

'ALBA' has white flowers. **EXCELSIOR HYBRIDS** come in pastel shades and are good flowers for cutting. **FOXY HYBRIDS** have carmine, pink, cream, or white flowers with flecks of maroon. Foxy hybrids are often grown as annual plants.

YELLOW FOXGLOVE *(D. grandiflora)* grows 4 to 6 feet tall and 2 feet wide. It has pale yellow blooms with brown veins.

STRAWBERRY FOXGLOVE *(D. × mertonensis)* is a perennial with strawberry-pink blooms. Divide it every two or three years for healthy, vigorous growth.

How to grow

PLANTING: Foxglove is easy to grow from seed or nursery-grown transplants. Plant it 18 inches apart in spring or fall. After planting, water deeply and add 3 inches of mulch around, but not touching, the plants.

CARE: Apply slow-release plant food at planting or begin using water-soluble plant food three weeks after planting in spring. ❶ Foxglove often needs staking to stand straight. Shortly after planting, sink a stake into the ground beside the plant. Use soft twine to tie the stem to the stake.

Remove flower stalks after blooms have faded. Or if you would like to harvest seeds for planting throughout the garden, leave bloom stalks standing. ❷ Harvest seeds after they dry on the stalk. If plants do not self-seed in the landscape, plan to replace them every year or two with container-grown stock.

PESTS: Diseases affecting foxglove include Southern blight, anthracnose, and fungal leaf spots. Pick off affected leaves. Water in the morning or use soaker hoses to avoid wetting the foliage. Remove and destroy plant debris in fall. Dig up and destroy rotted plants. Improve soil drainage and let soil dry between waterings.

Notes

_____

_____

_____

_____

< 49 >

GARDEN PHLOX (*Phlox paniculata*)

'DAVID' GARDEN PHLOX

'KATHERINE'

'LAURA'

'BRIGHT EYES'

FEATURES	
LIGHT: full sun to part shade	
SIZE: 4' tall by 2' to 3' wide	
WATER: 1" to 2" per week	
ZONES: 3–8	

> Large, showy flowers

> Long-blooming

> Disease-resistant cultivars available

From summer to early autumn, **GARDEN PHLOX** is topped with clusters of white, lavender, pink, or rose blue flowers. Some cultivars have fragrant blossoms. Garden phlox attracts bees and butterflies and is an excellent flower for cutting. This fast-growing perennial pairs well with speedwell, shrub roses, and daylilies.

SITE: Grow garden phlox in full sun or part shade and fertile, well-drained, moist soil. A planting spot with good air circulation is essential to discourage powdery mildew.

< 50 >

Recommended cultivars

'DAVID' has white flowers and resists disease. 'KATHERINE' has lavender flowers and is also disease resistant. 'BRIGHT EYES' has clear, pale pink flowers with red eyes. 'LAURA' stands up to wind and rarely needs staking. It has lavender flowers with white centers. 'LITTLE BOY' is disease resistant and has two-toned mauve and white flowers. 'BLUE PARADISE' bears purple-blue flowers.

How to grow

PLANTING: ❶ Plant garden phlox 24 to 36 inches apart in spring or fall. Take care to space plants adequately to promote good air circulation and discourage an outbreak of powdery mildew. Plant garden phlox in groups of at least three to five plants for the best effect.

CARE: Provide plants with 1 to 2 inches of water per week. ❷ Deadhead spent blooms to encourage reblooming and prevent self-seeding. Divide plants every three years in spring or fall to maintain their vigor. Cut plants to the ground in fall after frost disfigures the foliage.

PESTS: Phlox is susceptible to powdery mildew. Take care to select mildew-resistant cultivars. Keep the soil moist but not soggy. Overhead irrigation tends to spread disease, so water plants at the base of their stems. ❸ Maintain good air circulation by thinning dense clumps of garden phlox. Select three to five stems in the center of the clump and cut them back to the ground.

Notes

_____

_____

_____

_____

_____

_____

_____

< 51 >

HOLLYHOCK (*Alcea rosea*)

HOLLYHOCK

'NIGRA'

'CHATER'S DOUBLE'

'HAPPY LIGHTS'

FEATURES

LIGHT:	full sun
SIZE:	5' to 8' tall by 2' wide
WATER:	1" to 2" per week
ZONES:	3–9

> Cottage garden favorite

> Easy to grow

> Self-seeds freely

HOLLYHOCK'S tall stalks bear single or double flowers in shades of red, pink, white, purple, and yellow in midsummer. The plants self-seed and will spread throughout the garden. Good companions include shrub roses, black-eyed Susan, and ornamental grasses.

SITE: Grow hollyhock in full sun and fertile, well-drained soil. Disease and insect pests may disfigure hollyhock's foliage, so place it in the back of the border.

< 52 >

Recommended cultivars

'CHATER'S DOUBLE' has double flowers in
shades of maroon, red, rose, white, or yellow.
'HAPPY LIGHTS' blooms from early summer to
late fall and is rust resistant. 'NIGRA', also
called the 'Watchman', has single deep-
purplish-brown, almost black, blossoms.
'SUMMER CARNIVAL' has fully double,
peonylike flowers on 5-foot-tall stems.

How to grow

PLANTING: Plant hollyhocks 18 to 24 inches
apart in spring or fall.

CARE: Deadhead spent blossoms to encourage
reblooming. Remove diseased or disfigured
foliage. If you would like to harvest seed
from hollyhocks, do not deadhead. Allow the
blossoms to wither and seeds to form. ❶ Clip
seedpods just after they turn brown and dry.
❷ Store seeds in an airtight container. To
plant, sprinkle the seeds over soilless media and lightly cover. Or
direct-sow seeds in the garden. The seedlings will vary in appearance
from the original plant.

Plants require staking for flower stalks to stand straight and tall. Sink a
4- to 5-foot-tall stake in the ground beside the plant. Secure the stem to
the stake with soft twine.

Hollyhock is a short-lived perennial. Cut plants back to 6 inches above
the ground after blooming. In late fall, cut them all the way to the
ground and remove all diseased foliage and stems from the garden.

PESTS: Diseases that affect hollyhocks include hollyhock rust, Southern
blight, and bacterial and fungal leaf spots. Insect pests include flea
beetles, Japanese beetles, aphids, slugs, and leaf miners. The best defense
for these pests is to meet hollyhocks' cultural requirements (sun, water,
nutrients) and to plant disease-resistant cultivars.

Notes

_____

_____

_____

_____

< 53 >

'PATRIOT'

'HALCYON'

A MIX OF HOSTA CULTIVARS

'GOLD STANDARD'

FEATURES

LIGHT: partial to full shade	
SIZE: 2" to 48" tall by 2" to 48" wide	
WATER: 1" to 2" per week	
ZONES: 3–8	

> Easy to grow

> Attractive foliage

> Hundreds—maybe thousands—of varieties

HOSTA boasts mounds of heart-shaped, oval, or lance-shaped leaves in shades of green, blue, yellow, or white. Stalks of bell-shaped blue, lavender, or white flowers appear in summer; some cultivars have fragrant blooms. Interesting and low maintenance, hostas are classic choices for the perennial shade border.

Plant hostas in groups of three or five or more. Grow them in the border, in the woodland garden, in containers or at the base of woody plants. Good companions include astilbe, columbine, and ligularia.

SITE: Grow hosta in partial or full shade and fertile, moist, well-drained soil.

< **54** >

Recommended cultivars

Hundreds of hosta cultivars are available to suit  almost any shade gardener's preferences. Take care to select cultivars that are hardy in your area. **FORTUNE'S HOSTA** *(H. fortunei)* grows 24 inches tall and wide and has mounds of heart-shaped green to gray-green leaves. **LANCE LEAF HOSTA** *(H. lancifolia)* has pointed leaves that add drama to the edge of the border. **FRAGRANT HOSTA** *(H. plantaginea)* has large, heart-shaped yellowish-green leaves and sweetly  fragrant white flowers in late summer.

How to grow

PLANTING: ❶ Plant hostas in spring or fall 6 to 36 inches apart, depending on the cultivar's mature size.

CARE: Apply slow-release plant food at planting or begin using water-soluble plant food three weeks after planting in spring. When the soil feels dry 2 inches below the surface, water  hostas deeply. Mulch plants to help conserve soil moisture.

Many hostas are long-lived and do not require division to remain vigorous. ❷ If desired, divide hostas in spring or fall. Dig around the entire plant and lift it from the ground. Plunge a sharp spade through the crown and root system. Select pieces with healthy roots and shoots to reset in the garden. ❸ Cut the plants back in fall once frost withers the foliage.

PESTS: Slugs and snails disfigure hostas by boring holes into the leaves. If slug and snail damage is minor, control the pests by handpicking them at night and destroying. Eliminate their habitat by removing mulch from the area. If infestations are severe, use Ortho Bug-Geta Snail & Slug Killer.

Notes

_____

_____

_____

< 55 >

LADY'S MANTLE (*Alchemilla mollis*)

ALPINE LADY'S MANTLE

LADY'S MANTLE

DWARF LADY'S MANTLE

FEATURES	
LIGHT: full sun to part shade	
SIZE: 24" tall by 24" wide	
WATER: 1" to 2" per week	
ZONES: 3–7	

> Attractive, fuzzy leaves

> Good ground cover plant

From early summer until fall, tiny chartreuse blooms on wiry stems cover **LADY'S MANTLE**. The flowers float above green, velvety foliage. Plant lady's mantle in the front of the border or at the edge of a container to fully enjoy the blooms and foliage. The flowers are good for cutting and drying. Lovely garden companions include coral bells, astilbe, garden phlox, and salvia.

SITE: Grow lady's mantle in full sun and fertile, well-drained soil. In hot regions, plant it where it will receive morning sun and afternoon shade. It does not tolerate high humidity.

< 56 >

Recommended cultivars

ALPINE LADY'S MANTLE *(A. alpina)* grows just 6 inches tall and spreads slowly. It is hardy in Zones 5 to 7. **DWARF LADY'S MANTLE** *(A. erythropoda)* grows 9 inches tall and 12 inches wide. Its flowering stems often develop a red coloration. It is hardy in Zones 3 to 7.

How to grow

PLANTING: ❶ Plant lady's mantle 18 inches apart in spring or fall.

CARE: Apply a slow-release plant food at planting or begin using water-soluble plant food three weeks after planting. Deadhead spent blossoms to encourage reblooming. Divide plants every three years if desired. Sever the root system of this spreading plant with a sharp spade and reset portions with healthy roots and top shoots. Newly divided plants usually take a full year before they bloom on schedule.

Cut plants to the ground in late fall or leave them erect for winter interest. Cut these plants back in early spring.

PESTS: Four-lined plant bug occasionally feeds on the foliage of lady's mantle. Knock bugs off with a strong spray of water from the garden hose or apply an insecticide that is labeled for use on lady's mantle. Lady's mantle is also susceptible to spider mites. Spray insecticidal soap to control them.

Notes

_____
_____
_____
_____
_____
_____
_____
_____
_____
_____

< **57** >

LAMB'S-EARS *(Stachys byzantina)*

'SILVER CARPET'

'BIG EARS'

LAMB'S-EARS   'PRIMROSE HERON'

FEATURES

LIGHT:	full sun
SIZE:	18" tall by 24" wide
WATER:	1" per week
ZONES:	3–8

> Fuzzy, silver foliage

> Low maintenance

> Fast growing

> Deer and rabbit resistant

LAMB'S-EARS is prized for its aptly named soft, silvery velvety foliage, which is accompanied by spikes of woolly pink flowers from early summer to autumn. The flowers attract butterflies and bees. Lamb's-ears does well in the perennial border, as a ground cover, or as an accent in container plantings.

Good companions include garden phlox, thrift, roses, and sedum.

SITE: Grow lamb's-ears in full sun and moderately fertile, well-drained soil. Plants fare poorly in humid climates.

< 58 >

Recommended cultivars

'SILVER CARPET' is a nonflowering, low-maintenance cultivar with a tidy habit. 'BIG EARS' has large silver-green leaves and rarely blooms. It is sometimes sold as 'HELENE VON STEIN'. The flowers of 'COTTON BOLL' cluster along the stem and resemble cotton balls. 'MARGERY FISH' has mauve flowers. 'PRIMROSE HERON' has yellow-green leaves.

How to grow

PLANTING: Plant lamb's-ears 18 to 24 inches apart in spring or fall.

CARE: Apply slow-release plant food in spring. Or use a water-soluble plant food once a month; cease feeding six to eight weeks prior to the first frost date. Groom plants regularly to remove brown or diseased foliage from the thick mat of leaves. Several cultivars do not require grooming. Some gardeners find lamb's-ears flowers unattractive and cut them off at ground level as soon as they appear.

Divide lamb's-ears in spring or autumn at least every three years to maintain vigor and control growth. ❶ Dig the root ball and lift it out of the ground. ❷ Pull or cut apart the clump. ❸ Reset the pieces that have healthy roots and shoots. Prune the plant back in fall once frost withers the foliage.

PESTS: Powdery mildew occasionally troubles lamb's-ears. Select mildew-resistant cultivars and provide adequate air circulation. Plants are apt to die over winter in poorly drained sites.

Notes

_____
_____
_____
_____
_____

< 59 >

LAVENDER *(Lavandula angustifolia)*

'HIDCOTE'

'JEAN DAVIS'

LAVENDER 'MUNSTEAD'

FEATURES	
LIGHT: full sun	
SIZE: 2' to 3' tall and wide	
WATER: 1" per week	
ZONES: 5–8	

> Fragrant flowers and foliage

> Tolerates drought

> Flowers good for drying

LAVENDER is a woody shrub with silvery leaves that complement many perennial plants. The leaves contain volatile oils, which account for the classic lavender scent. In summer, fragrant flowers spikes appear. They attract bees and butterflies and are excellent freshly cut or dried.

Plant lavender near the front of the perennial border. Good garden companions include spike speedwell, sedum, and roses.

SITE: Grow lavender in full sun and well-drained soil. The soil must drain freely for lavender to thrive. If you have poorly drained soil, plant lavender in containers or raised beds. Lavender is an excellent choice for hot, dry locations.

< **60** >

Recommended cultivars

'HIDCOTE' grows 24 inches tall and has deep purple flowers and a compact, tidy habit. 'MUNSTEAD' grows 18 inches tall and has blue-purple flowers. 'NANA ALBA' has white flowers. 'ROSEA', 'JEAN DAVIS', and 'LODDON PINK' have light pink flowers.

How to grow

PLANTING: Plant lavender 18 to 24 inches apart in spring. Apply slow-release plant food at planting.

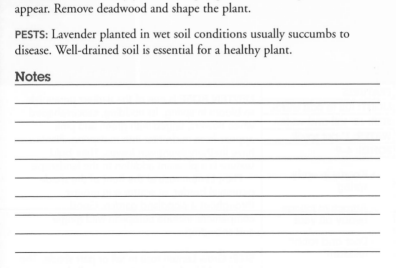

CARE: Deadhead spent blooms to encourage reblooming. ❶ Shear the plant back to 8 inches above the ground after the first flowering to promote a compact habit.

To dry lavender, clip flower stalks before they fully open and secure in 1-inch diameter or smaller bundles. ❷ Hang the bundles upside down in a dry, shaded area. When the bundles are dry, place them in an airtight container until you are ready to use them.

Prune lavender every year in late spring. Wait for new growth to appear. Remove deadwood and shape the plant.

PESTS: Lavender planted in wet soil conditions usually succumbs to disease. Well-drained soil is essential for a healthy plant.

Notes

_____

_____

_____

_____

_____

_____

_____

_____

_____

_____

_____

< 61 >

LENTEN ROSE *(Helleborus orientalis)*

'ROYAL HERITAGE' HYBRID

'SUNSHINE FARM' HYBRID

LENTEN ROSE | BEAR'S FOOT HELLEBORE

FEATURES

LIGHT: full to part shade

SIZE: 18" tall and wide

WATER: 1" per week

ZONES: 4–9

> Blooms in early spring

> Attractive foliage nearly all year

> Deer and rabbit resistant

LENTEN ROSE is one of the earliest perennials to bloom in spring. Its nodding, saucer-shaped white flowers, tinged with green and pink, appear from midwinter into midspring. Plants have leathery evergreen leaves. Their bold texture is a pleasant addition to the landscape.

Plant Lenten rose at the front of the shade perennial border, or scatter it in groups throughout a woodland garden. Good companions include European wild ginger and snowdrop.

SITE: Grow Lenten rose in full or part shade. The soil should be fertile, moist, and well-drained.

< **62** >

Recommended cultivars

Many hybrids have been developed offering flowers in a broad palette of colors and forms. 'BLUE LADY' has large, dark burgundy flowers. Those of 'MRS. BETTY RANICAR' are large, clear-white and double. MILLET HYBRIDS have larger, 2- to 3-inch-wide white, pink, or red flowers. CAUCASICAN ORIENTAL LENTEN ROSE (H. o. abchasicus) has pale green flowers marked with reddish-purple on the outside.

BEAR'S FOOT HELLEBORE (H. foetidus) has nodding, bell-shaped green flowers, sometimes with a purple rim, from midwinter to midspring. Its lobed, deep green leaves smell putrid when crushed but are handsome additions to the shady landscape.

CHRISTMAS ROSE (H. niger) has saucer-shaped white flowers, sometimes tinged with pale pink and green. They appear from early winter to early spring.

How to grow

PLANTING: Plant Lenten rose 18 inches apart in spring or fall.

CARE: Apply slow-release plant food at planting or begin using water-soluble plant food three weeks after planting in spring. Lenten rose self-sows in the landscape. If you desire, move the seedlings before surrounding plants shade them out; seedlings take three or four years to reach mature size. There is no need to prune back plants in fall because the foliage is evergreen. ❶ In spring, trim off tattered and winter-damaged leaves.

PESTS: Plants are relatively pest-free when given their cultural requirements (light, water, nutrients).

Notes

_____
_____
_____
_____
_____
_____

< 63 >

'STAR GAZER' ORIENTAL LILY

'CHIPPEWA STAR' ASIATIC LILY

TRUMPET LILY

TURK'S-CAP LILY

FEATURES	
LIGHT: full sun to part shade	
SIZE: 2' to 4' tall by 1' wide	
WATER: 1" per week	
ZONES: 3–8	

> Spectacular blooms in midsummer

> Flowers available in a variety of shapes and colors

> Low maintenance

Blooming **LILIES** instantly light up the garden with their big, bold flowers in a rainbow of hues. Often fragrant, the flowers are available in many shapes, depending on the species. From the traditional cup-shaped flowers to trumpet-shaped blooms to those with recurved petals, there is a lily for every garden style.

For the best effect, plant lilies in groups of five, seven, or nine. Good companions include lady's mantle, roses, and clematis.

SITE: Grow lilies in full sun and fertile, well-drained soil.

< **64** >

Recommended cultivars

ASIATIC LILIES grow 2 to 5 feet tall with 4- to 6-inch cup-shape blooms in red, yellow, orange, pink, white, or lavender. Flowers may face up, out, or down. **ORIENTAL LILIES** have fragrant, bowl-shape blooms with recurved petals in white, red, pink, or bicolors. Plants grow 2 to 8 feet tall. Pink-flowering 'Star Gazer' is one of the most popular. **TRUMPET LILIES** reach 4 to 6 feet tall and have 6- to 10-inch-long trumpet-shape blooms in gold, cream, or rose. 'Golden Splendor' has large, scented, golden-yellow flowers. The long branched stems of **TURK'S-CAP LILY** (*L. superbum*) bear up to 40 unscented flowers with recurved petals from mid- to late summer.

How to grow

PLANTING: Lilies grow from scaly bulbs. In fall or early spring, plant bulbs 6 to 12 inches apart and two to three times deeper than their diameter.

CARE: Staking is often needed to keep lilies upright, especially the tallest species. ❶ When plants are 4 to 5 inches tall, sink a stake into the ground about 4 inches from the stem. Tie the stem to the stake with soft twine. As plants grow, continue tying plants to the stake. ❷ You can also use twigs and branches to prop

up plants. Deadhead spent flowers to direct the plant's energy into developing a strong bulb. Allow the foliage to die back naturally after the blooms fade. ❸ In fall, cut back frost-nipped foliage to the ground.

PESTS: Deer, rabbits, and groundhogs may eat the stems and flower buds. Cover plants to discourage these animals. Snails and slugs also occasionally dine on the foliage. Destroy their habitat by removing mulch from the planting area.

Notes

_____

_____

_____

< 65 >

NEW ENGLAND ASTER *(Aster novae-angliae)*

NEW ENGLAND ASTER

NEW YORK ASTER

'MONCH'

CALICO ASTER

FEATURES	
LIGHT: full sun	
SIZE: 2' to 5' tall by 4' wide	
WATER: 1" per week	
ZONES: 4–8	

> Blooms in late
  summer and fall

> Attractive rounded
  habit

NEW ENGLAND ASTER is a good plant for cottage gardens, wetland areas, or, if cut back to promote compact growth, containers. Violet daisies with yellow centers cover plants from late summer to midautumn.

Its flowers attract butterflies and are excellent for cutting. Good companions include Russian sage, ornamental grasses, and black-eyed Susan.

SITE: Grow New England aster in full sun and fertile, moist soil.

< 66 >

Recommended cultivars

'ALMA POTSCHKE' blooms in rose-red and reaches 3 to 4 feet tall. NEW YORK ASTER (A. novi-belgii) grows 1 to 6 feet tall and 3 feet wide and has violet flowers from late summer into fall. Zones 4 to 8. FRIKART'S ASTER (A. × frikartii) is a loose, 3-foot-tall plant. Zones 5 to 8. 'MONCH' has long-lasting lavender blooms. CALICO ASTER (A. lateriflorus) is a 3-foot, dark-leaved aster with tiny white flowers.

How to grow

PLANTING: ❶ Plant New England aster 18 to 24 inches apart in spring or fall.

CARE: Apply slow-release plant food at planting or begin using water-soluble plant food three weeks after planting in spring. New England aster tolerates dry soil once established but performs better in moist soils.

❷ Water deeply when soil begins to dry out. Don't be discouraged if lower leaves drop during the summer. This is common and does not harm the plant's health. ❸ To promote compact growth, pinch or cut back plants by 3 inches when they are 6 inches tall. Cut back again by one-half in midsummer. If not pinched, New England aster will probably need staking to remain upright.

Divide plants every two years in spring or fall to maintain vigor and control growth.

PESTS: Powdery mildew and fungal leaf spot are common problems. Apply regular fungicide treatments to control these diseases unless the plant is at the rear of the border where the foliage is not readily visible.

Notes

_____
_____
_____
_____
_____

< 67 >

ORIENTAL POPPY *(Papaver orientale)*

'ALLEGRO'

'BLACK AND WHITE'

ORIENTAL POPPY | 'PATTY'S PLUM'

FEATURES	
LIGHT: full sun	
SIZE: 18" to 36" tall by 24" to 36" wide	
WATER: 1" per week	
ZONES: 3–7	

> Large papery petals

> Short but spectacular flower display

ORIENTAL POPPY'S fabulous red, orange, pink, or white flowers open in mid- to late spring but finish blooming all too soon. Because the plants go dormant after they bloom, combine them with later-emerging perennials to hide their fading foliage. Good companions for oriental poppy include Russian sage, New England aster, and daylily.

SITE: Grow oriental poppy in full sun and deep, fertile, well-drained soil. Plants prefer cool temperatures and dislike heat and humidity. They do not do well in windy sites or in wet soil.

< 68 >

Recommended cultivars

'ALLEGRO' has red-orange flowers marked with black at the base of the petals. 'BEAUTY OF LIVERMERE' bears red flowers up to 8 inches across. 'BLACK AND WHITE' has white flowers with a reddish-black stain at the base. 'CARNIVAL' bears crinkly red-orange flowers stained with white at the base.

How to grow

PLANTING: Plant oriental poppies 24 inches apart in spring or fall. Apply slow-release plant food at planting in spring.

CARE: Oriental poppies usually go dormant in summer, so don't worry that your plants have died. They will return in the fall. Division is not necessary for good growth, but you can divide plants in summer while they are dormant if you would like new starts. Dig around the clump with a spade, then lift the entire plant from the soil. Use the spade or a knife to split the clump. Wash the soil from each division. Each should have a stem or growing point and a few roots. ❶ Dig a hole that is as wide as the spread-out roots. Form a cone in the bottom of the hole. ❷ Set the division on the cone and spread the roots uniformly over it, then check the depth of the plant. The bottom of the division's stem should be level with your spade handle. ❸ Cover the division with soil leaving just its "nose" sticking out.

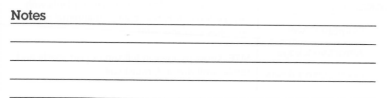

PESTS: Botrytis, powdery mildew, and root rot sometimes trouble oriental poppy.

Notes

_____
_____
_____
_____
_____

< 69 >

PEONY *(Paeonia officinalis)*

'BLUSHING PRINCESS'

'KANSAS'

'PILLOW TALK'

PEONY

FEATURES
LIGHT: full sun to part shade
SIZE: 24" to 36" tall and wide
WATER: 1" per week
ZONES: 3–8

> Fragrant flowers

> Attractive foliage

> Good cutting flower

PEONIES thrive for decades, sending up fragrant, petal-packed blooms year after year in late spring. Dark green foliage complements the pink, white, red, or lilac flowers and provides a wonderful backdrop, filler, and support for later-blooming perennials.

Combine these low-maintenance plants with iris, garden phlox, bee balm, ornamental grasses and New England aster.

SITE: Grow peonies in full sun or part shade and fertile, well-drained, moist soil.

< 70 >

Recommended cultivars

Hundreds of named peony cultivars exist. Grow several and enjoy a diversity of flower colors and shapes. TREE PEONY *(P. suffruticosa)* grows 7 feet tall and 3 to 4 feet wide. It has large white, red, pink, or purple flowers in late spring. Its woody stems create a graceful scene in the winter landscape. Zones 4 to 7.

How to grow

PLANTING: Plant peonies 24 to 36 inches apart in early fall. ❶ Ensure that the eyes, or growing points, are just 2 inches below the soil surface. Peonies planted deeper than 2 inches will not bloom; those planted too close to the surface are apt to freeze. Add bonemeal and slow-release plant food to the soil at planting. ❷ Water thoroughly.

CARE: For best growth, provide peonies with 1 inch of water per week. To prevent the heavy flowers from pulling down the stems and lying on the ground, set grow-through stakes over plants in early spring. ❸ After flowers fade, cut off spent blooms and seedpods.

Cut stems and leaves to the ground after frost disfigures the foliage. Remove and store grow-through stakes until springtime. If disease was present, disinfect the stakes and pruning tools and dispose of all trimmed foliage.

PESTS: Numerous problems affect peonies, especially ones growing in wet soil. Botrytis blight is one of the most common, causing dark spots on the leaves. Remove and destroy affected leaves. Cut back plants in fall and remove the debris. Plant in a well-drained location.

Notes

_____

_____

_____

_____

< 71 >

PERENNIAL SALVIA

'MAY NIGHT'

'ROSE QUEEN'

'EAST FRIESLAND'

FEATURES	
LIGHT: full sun	
SIZE: 24" to 36" tall by 18" to 24" wide	
WATER: 1" per week	
ZONES: 5–9	

> Long-blooming flowers

> Low maintenance

PERENNIAL SALVIA bears brilliant spires of violet or purple flowers from midsummer through early autumn. It attracts bees and butterflies. Plant perennial salvia in groups in the border or use it in container plantings. Good companions include black-eyed Susan, yarrow, New England aster, and ornamental grasses.

SITE: Grow perennial salvia in full sun and moderately fertile, well-drained soil.

< 72 >

Recommended cultivars

'MAY NIGHT' has large indigo-blue flowers on  18-inch-tall stems. 'ROSE QUEEN' has rose-pink flowers and gray-tinted leaves. 'EAST FRIESLAND' has deep reddish-purple spikes.

COMMON SAGE *(S. officinalis)*, with its silvery leaves enhances perennial borders and containers as well as herb gardens. 'AUREA' grows 12 inches tall and bears golden-yellow leaves.

How to grow

PLANTING: Plant perennial salvia 18 inches apart in spring or fall.

CARE: Apply slow-release plant food in spring. ❶ Deadhead spent blooms to encourage reblooming. Cut plants back to 10 to 12 inches in height after flowering to encourage another flush of flowers. You can cut each flower stem individually or use hedge clippers to shear plants. Prune foliage back to 6 inches tall once frost withers the foliage.

Divide perennial salvia in spring every three years to maintain its vigor. Dig around the root clump and lift. Use a sharp spade to slice through the root system. Reset portions that contain healthy roots and shoots.

PESTS: Diseases include powdery mildew, rust, stem rot, and fungal leaf spots. Poorly drained soil leads to most perennial salvia diseases. For best growth, improve soil with compost prior to planting.

Notes

_____
_____
_____
_____
_____
_____
_____
_____
_____

< 73 >

PURPLE CONEFLOWER

'KIM'S KNEE HIGH'

'MAGNUS'

'ORANGE MEADOWBRITE'

FEATURES

LIGHT:	full sun
SIZE:	2' to 4' tall by 1' to 2' wide
WATER:	1" per week
ZONES:	3–9

> Attracts butterflies

> Drought tolerant

> Good cutting flower

Long-blooming **PURPLE CONEFLOWER** is a sturdy addition to the perennial garden. Its purple daisies with orange or brown cone-shaped centers appear from midsummer to autumn. Plants are magnificent in the full-sun border or in mixed container plantings. The flowers are excellent for cutting. Good companion plants include ornamental grasses, Russian sage, and stonecrop.

SITE: Purple coneflower grows well in full sun and fertile, well-drained soil.

< **74** >

Recommended cultivars

'MAGNUS' has large, flat, bright purple flowers with deep orange disks. 'ROBERT BLOOM' has rich crimson-tinted mauve flowers with deep orange-brown disks. Those of 'FINALE WHITE' have greenish-brown disks. 'KIM'S KNEE HIGH' is a 20-inch-tall cultivar with large purple flowers. ORANGE MEADOWBRITE has deep orange flowers and a sweet orange tea fragrance. MANGO MEADOWBRITE has yellow flowers. Flowers of 'WHITE SWAN' are white, honey-scented, and have orange-brown centers.

How to grow

PLANTING: Plant purple coneflower 18 inches apart in early spring or fall.

CARE: Apply slow-release plant food at planting or begin using water-soluble plant food three weeks after planting in spring. Deadhead by cutting spent flower stalks back to the ground to stimulate rebloom. Plants moderately self-seed in the landscape. Seedlings are easy to transplant or remove if unwanted.

Divide purple coneflower in fall or early spring. ❶ Dig around the root clump and lift. ❷ Use a sharp spade to slice through the root system. Reset portions that contain healthy roots and shoots. Prune plants back after frost withers the foliage.

PESTS: Purple coneflower is relatively pest-free when planted in moderately fertile soil. Powdery mildew, aster yellows, and bacterial leaf spots may occur but are rarely serious.

Notes

_____
_____
_____
_____
_____
_____
_____
_____

< 75 >

RUSSIAN SAGE

'BLUE SPIRE'

'FILAGRAN'

'LONGIN'

FEATURES

LIGHT:	full sun
SIZE:	4' tall by 4' wide
WATER:	drought tolerant
ZONES:	3–9

> Heat tolerant

> Silver foliage with fine texture

> Flowers attract bees and butterflies

Lavender flowers adorn **RUSSIAN SAGE** from summer into fall. The silver-green, finely cut foliage forms a broad airy column in the garden. Like lavender, Russian sage is a woody shrub. Plant it at the back of the garden or grow it in large containers. Good companions include black-eyed Susan, purple coneflower, ornamental grasses, and stonecrop.

SITE: Grow Russian sage in full sun and moderately fertile, well-drained soil.

< **76** >

Recommended cultivars

'BLUE MIST' begins blooming in early summer and has light blue flowers. 'BLUE SPIRE' bears finely cut leaves and deep lavender-blue flowers. 'LONGIN' has an upright habit. 'FILAGRAN' has pale blue flowers and foliage that is even more finely divided. 'LITTLE SPIRE' grows just 2 feet tall.

How to grow

PLANTING: Plant Russian sage 24 to 36 inches apart in spring or fall. Apply a slow-release plant food at planting.

CARE: Water Russian sage only when the soil is dry 2 to 3 inches below the surface. Plants are self-cleaning, so deadheading is not necessary. ❶ Prune plants yearly in spring after they have begun growing. Remove dead stems and shape plants. If plants become unkempt or overgrown, you can rejuvenate them as you would a shrub. ❷ To rejuvenate, trim woody stems back almost to the ground in spring.

Russian sage may require staking in moist, rich soil. Use grow-through supports to keep plants upright.

PESTS: Plants are relatively pest-free when given their cultural requirements (sun, soil, planting depth, moisture).

Notes

_____

_____

_____

_____

_____

_____

_____

< 77 >

SEDUM *(Sedum spectabile)*

'MATRONA'

'FROSTY MORN'

'AUTUMN JOY'   'VERA JAMESON'

FEATURES

LIGHT:	full sun
SIZE:	2' tall and wide
WATER:	1" per week
ZONES:	3–10

> Succulent foliage

> Long-lasting fall flowers

> Attracts bees and butterflies

SEDUMS are sturdy, succulent late-blooming perennials. The species has pink flowers; cultivars and hybrid sedums offer deeper, richer flower colors. Foliage is attractive throughout the growing season and bears long-lasting flowers in late summer and fall. The flowers open pink in mid- to late summer, then turn rose-red, then deep brown-burgundy in late autumn. Good companions include purple coneflower, ornamental grasses, and black-eyed Susan.

SITE: Plant sedum in full sun and moderately fertile, well-drained soil.

< **78** >

Recommended cultivars

'AUTUMN JOY' flowers open pink in mid- to late summer, then turn rose-red, then brownish burgundy in late fall. 'RUBY GLOW' grows 12 inches tall and 18 inches wide and has red stems, bronze-tinged green leaves, and ruby-red flowers from midsummer to early fall. 'PURPLE EMPEROR' has dark bronze or burgundy foliage and rose-red flowers. 'FROSTY MORN' has white-edged leaves and pink flowers. 'MATRONA' has purplish gray-green leaves, red stems, and dark pink flowers. 'VERA JAMESON' has purple-bronze foliage and pink blooms; it grows only 1 foot tall.

How to grow

PLANTING: Plant 'Autumn Joy' sedum 18 to 24 inches apart in spring or fall.

CARE: Divide plants growing in moderately fertile soil every three years to maintain form and vigor. In rich soils plan to divide sedum more frequently. Floppy stems signal that it's time to divide. Note: Lack of sun also causes stems to fall over.

❶ To divide, dig around the root clump and lift. ❷ Use your spade, a trowel, or a knife to slice through the root system. The larger the portion, the larger the new plant will be during the first year. Smaller pieces may take two to three years to reach mature size and bloom. ❸ Reset portions that contain healthy roots and top shoots. Discard any dead pieces.

Prune sedum back in fall or leave it in the garden for winter enjoyment and cut back in early spring.

PESTS: Sedum is relatively pest-free when given its cultural requirements (sun, soil, planting depth, moisture).

Notes

_____

_____

_____

< 79 >

SHASTA DAISY *(Leucanthemum × superbum)*

'ALASKA'

'WIRRAL'S PRIDE'

SHASTA DAISY   'BECKY'

FEATURES	
LIGHT: full sun to part shade	
SIZE: 36" tall by 24" wide	
WATER: 1" per week	
ZONES: 4–8	

> Classic white daisy

> Excellent cutting flower

> Deer resistant

Reliable and cheerful white-and-yellow flowers decorate **SHASTA DAISY** in early summer; if you deadhead before seeds form, you may have flowers through early autumn. The blooms make long-lasting cut flowers. Plants are well-suited for the perennial border or the container. Good companions include roses, lamb's-ears, threadleaf coreopsis, and bee balm.

SITE: Grow shasta daisy in full sun or part shade and moderately fertile, well-drained soil.

< 80 >

Recommended cultivars

'MARCONI' has striking double flowers and thrives in part shade. 'ALASKA' has single flowers. 'BECKY' grows especially well in hot, humid areas, blooming for weeks.

How to grow

PLANTING: Plant shasta daisies 18 to 24 inches apart in spring or fall. Apply slow-release plant food at planting.

CARE: ❶ Deadhead spent blooms by cutting flower stalks back to the dense foliage to encourage rebloom.

Clumps of shasta daisy tend to die out in the center. Divide plants every two to three years in spring or fall. ❷ To divide, dig around the clump and lift it out of the ground. Slice through the root system with the spade. Discard unhealthy portions of the clump and cut the remaining parts into sections. The larger the portion, the larger the resulting plant during the first year. Small pieces may take two to three years to reach mature size and bloom. ❸ Replant portions that contain healthy roots and top shoots.

Prune back shasta daisy plants once frost withers the foliage.

PESTS: Diseases that trouble shasta daisy include crown gall, powdery mildew, leaf spots, and rust. Spray plants with Ortho Garden Disease Control Concentrate. Ensure good air circulation around and through plants. Aphids, spider mites, and slugs may also be problems. Blast aphids and mites with a sharp stream of water or use insecticidal soap. Apply Ortho Bug-Geta Slug and Snail Killer.

Notes

< 81 >

SILVER MOUND ARTEMISIA (*A. schmidtiana* 'Nana')

'SILVER BROCADE'

'POWIS CASTLE'

SILVER MOUND ARTEMISIA   WHITE SAGE

FEATURES	
LIGHT: full sun	
SIZE: 12" tall by 18" wide	
WATER: drought tolerant	
ZONES: 4–8	

> Showy silver foliage

SILVER MOUND ARTEMISIA has soft, fragrant silvery-green foliage that grows in a mound. Tiny yellow flowers appear in summer. Plants are well suited for the edge of a sunny border, a rock garden, or spilling over the sides of a container. The silver foliage is useful among bright-colored flowering plants. Good companions include yarrow, perennial salvia, and spike speedwell.

SITE: Grow silver mound artemisia in full sun and well-drained, average or moderately fertile soil. In hot areas it will tolerate light afternoon shade.

< 82 >

Recommended cultivars

There are several other excellent artemisia hybrids and species. 'SILVER BROCADE' (A. stelleriana) has broadly toothed silver leaves. It is a good ground cover artemisia. 'POWIS CASTLE' forms a dense 3- to 4-foot-tall clump of silvery-gray leaves. It is hardy in Zones 7 to 9. 'LAMBROOK SILVER' (A. absinthium) grows 2½ feet tall and has silky silver-gray leaves. WHITE SAGE (A. ludoviciana) has silvery-white leaves and reaches 4 feet tall by 24 feet wide. It is often invasive.

How to grow

PLANTING: Plant silver mound artemisia 15 to 18 inches apart in spring or fall.

CARE: Apply slow-release plant food at planting, or begin using water-soluble plant food three weeks after planting in spring. ❶ Shear silver mound artemisia to 6 inches tall after it blooms to restore the smooth-looking habit. If not sheared the foliage may become untidy. Water deeply only when the soil is dry; plants do poorly in constantly wet soil.

They also prefer a relatively infertile site. Stems will fall over, opening up the centers, if soil is too rich. In such situations, divide plants more frequently. In less fertile soil they can go three or more years without division. Divide plants in spring or fall. Cut plants to the ground in late fall or leave the stems for winter interest and cut them back in early spring before growth begins.

PESTS: Plants are relatively pest-free when given their cultural preferences (light, soil, water).

Notes

_____

_____

_____

_____

_____

_____

_____

_____

< 83 >

SPIDERWORT (*Tradescantia* hybrids)

SPIDERWORT

'ANGEL EYES'

'SWEET KATE'

'ZWANENBERG'

FEATURES	
LIGHT: full sun to part shade	
SIZE: 18" to 24" tall by 18" to 24" wide	
WATER: 1" per week	
ZONES: 4–9	

> Long blooming

> Attractive foliage

A North America native, **SPIDERWORT** sports cheerful three-petaled flowers in blue, purple, pink, or white from early summer to early autumn. Plant spiderwort in the cottage garden or bright woodland garden, or use it in container plantings. Good companions include roses, lamb's-ears, iris, and columbine.

SITE: Grow spiderwort in full sun or part shade and moderately fertile, well-drained, moist soil.

< 84 >

Recommended cultivars

'ALBA' bears white flowers. 'BLUE STONE' has blue flowers. 'CAERULEA PLENA' bears double blue flowers. 'IRIS PRITCHARD' has pale blue-tinged white flowers. 'SWEET KATE' has eye-catching yellow-green foliage and pale purple blooms. 'KARMINGLUT' has red flowers. 'ANGEL EYES' bears white flowers with light lavender-blue centers. 'PUREWELL GIANT' has purplish-pink flowers. 'ZWANENBERG' is a dark purple bloomer.

How to grow

PLANTING: ❶ Plant spiderwort 18 to 24 inches apart in spring or fall.

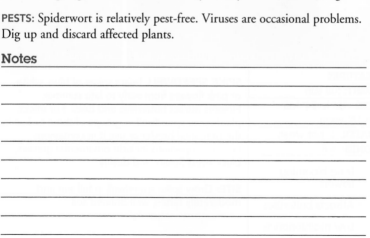

CARE: Plants will flop or fall open in rich soil or when fertilized with high-nitrogen plant foods. Feed spiderwort minimally. Spiderwort also tends to fall open after flowering. After the first flush of flowers, shear plants to promote a compact habit and encourage reblooming. Spiderwort is self-cleaning and does not need regular deadheading to look attractive. ❷ Deadheading, however, is useful in eliminating self-sown seedlings. Divide in spring or autumn at least every three years to maintain vigor.

PESTS: Spiderwort is relatively pest-free. Viruses are occasional problems. Dig up and discard affected plants.

Notes

_____
_____
_____
_____
_____
_____
_____
_____
_____
_____
_____

< 85 >

'RED FOX'

'SUNNY BORDER BLUE'

'GOODNESS GROWS'

SPIKE SPEEDWELL, LAMB'S-EARS AND ROSES

FEATURES	
LIGHT: full sun	
SIZE: 12" to 24" tall by 18" wide	
WATER: 1" per week	
ZONES: 3–8	

> Long-blooming flowers

> Attracts butterflies

> Low maintenance

SPIKE SPEEDWELL bears spires of blue, white, or pink flowers from early to late summer. Flowers attract butterflies and bees. For effect, plant spike speedwell in groups of three or five in the perennial border or use it in containers. Good companions include ornamental grasses, black-eyed Susan, and daylily.

SITE: Grow spike speedwell in full sun and moderately fertile, well-drained soil.

< 86 >

Recommended cultivars

'ALBA' has white flowers. 'BLUE FOX' bears deep blue flowers, while those of 'RED FOX' are rosy-red. 'ERICA' blooms in pink. 'MINUET' grows 10 inches tall and has pink flowers in late spring and silvery-gray leaves. 'GOODNESS GROWS' bears long dark blue flowers all summer and grows 10 inches tall.

'SUNNY BORDER BLUE' is a low-maintenance optimum performer that grows 18 inches tall and 12 to 15 inches wide and bears violet-blue flowers all summer.

How to grow

PLANTING: Plant spike speedwell 15 to 18 inches apart in spring or autumn.

CARE: ❶ In spring set a grow-through support or other staking system over plants and apply slow-release plant food. Mulch in summer to reduce weed seed germination, hold moisture in the soil, and, as it decomposes, add organic matter to the soil. Water deeply when the soil is dry. Deadhead spent blooms to encourage reblooming. ❷ Shear back leggy plants to 6 to 8 inches tall in midsummer.

Divide in spring or autumn at least every three years to maintain vigor. Prune back spike speedwell after frost withers the foliage.

PESTS: Plants are relatively pest-free when given their cultural conditions (sun, soil, planting depth, moisture). Root rot may occur in wet soils.

Notes

_____

_____

_____

_____

_____

_____

_____

_____

_____

_____

< 87 >

THREADLEAF COREOPSIS *(Coreopsis verticillata)*

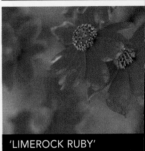

'MOONBEAM' & 'ZAGREB'

'LIMEROCK RUBY'

'ZAGREB' THREADLEAF COREOPSIS

PINK COREOPSIS

FEATURES	
LIGHT: full sun	
SIZE: 24" to 32" tall by 18" wide	
WATER: drought tolerant	
ZONES: 3–9	

> Easy to grow

> Blooms from early summer through fall

THREADLEAF COREOPSIS is a mass of delicate, petite yellow, pink, or red flowers from early summer until fall. True to its name, threadleaf coreopsis has attractive, finely textured foliage. Place it in the front of the perennial border or add it to a mixed container planting. Good companions include yarrow, black-eyed Susan, and daylily.

SITE: Grow threadleaf coreopsis in full sun and fertile, well-drained soil. Plants tolerate humidity and heat.

< 88 >

Recommended cultivars

'**MOONBEAM**', a superior selection that grows 18 inches tall and wide, has pale-yellow blooms from summer through autumn. '**ZAGREB**' has golden yellow flowers. '**LIMEROCK RUBY**' has pink-red flowers and finely textured foliage. It is hardy only to Zone 7 or warmer. **PINK COREOPSIS** *(C. rosea)* has fine texture, a neat habit, and pink blooms on and off all summer into fall.

How to grow

PLANTING: Plant threadleaf coreopsis 18 inches apart in spring or fall. Apply slow-release plant food at planting.

CARE: Water threadleaf coreopsis deeply when the soil is dry; allow the soil to dry between waterings. Apply 3 inches of mulch and reapply when necessary to maintain the 3-inch depth in summer and winter.

Threadleaf coreopsis is self-cleaning and does not need deadheading. If plants get leggy and flop, cut back by half their height to encourage compact growth.

Divide plants every three years or so in spring or early fall. ❶ Dig around the root clump and ❷ lift the plant of out the ground. ❸ Use a sharp spade to slice through the root system. Reset portions that contain healthy roots and top shoots.

Leave plants standing in fall until frost knocks them down, then cut them back in spring.

PESTS: Except for rabbits, plants are relatively pest-free when their cultural requirements (light, soil, moisture) are met.

Notes

_____

_____

_____

_____

_____

< **89** >

'FANAL' AND 'TAYGETEA'

'CERISE QUEEN'

YARROW   'MOONSHINE'

FEATURES	
LIGHT: full sun	
SIZE: 36" tall by 18" wide	
WATER: drought tolerant	
ZONES: 3–9	

> Deer and rabbit resistant

> Showy, long-lasting flowers

YARROW makes a blanket of golden yellow, flat-top flowers that open in early summer and last until autumn. Cut and dry the sturdy flowers for a long-lasting indoor arrangement. When not in bloom, the plant bears soft, silvery green, ferny foliage that hugs the ground. A fast-growing perennial, yarrow pairs well with false indigo, bellflower, and purple coneflower.

SITE: Yarrow does well in heat and takes occasional drought. It thrives in full sun and prefers well-drained, moderately fertile soil.

< 90 >

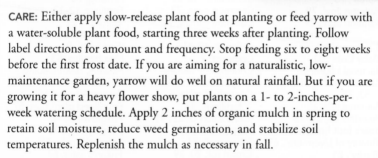

Recommended cultivars

'CORONATION GOLD' is a popular hybrid that grows 3 feet tall and has 4-inch-wide, golden-yellow flowers. Its flowers are excellent for drying. 'ALTGOLD' grows 2 to 3 feet tall and will rebloom if you remove faded flowers.

COMMON YARROW *(Achillea millefolium)* blooms in red, white, or pink and has dark green, low-growing foliage. It is vigorous and invasive. Better-mannered cultivars include 'FIRE KING', 'CERISE QUEEN', and 'RED BEAUTY'. 'MOONSHINE' is a hybrid yarrow that is slightly shorter than 'CORONATION GOLD'; it has pale yellow flowers.

How to grow

PLANTING: Plant yarrow 18 inches apart in spring or fall.

CARE: Either apply slow-release plant food at planting or feed yarrow with a water-soluble plant food, starting three weeks after planting. Follow label directions for amount and frequency. Stop feeding six to eight weeks before the first frost date. If you are aiming for a naturalistic, low-maintenance garden, yarrow will do well on natural rainfall. But if you are growing it for a heavy flower show, put plants on a 1- to 2-inches-per-week watering schedule. Apply 2 inches of organic mulch in spring to retain soil moisture, reduce weed germination, and stabilize soil temperatures. Replenish the mulch as necessary in fall.

❶ Deadhead spent blooms to encourage reblooming, cutting them at the base of the flower stalk. Cut blossoms are good in flower arrangements, and they dry well. Dried flowers hold their color longest when harvested soon after the flowers open. Cut flower stems to the ground in late fall or, for winter interest, leave them in place, then cut them back in early spring.

PESTS: Yarrow sometimes develops powdery mildew. Spacing plants at least 18 inches apart allows air circulation to help prevent the disease.

Notes

_____

_____

_____

_____

< 91 >

INDEX

< **92** >

< 93 >

< **94** >

This map of climate zones helps you select plants for your garden that will survive a typical winter in your region. The United States Department of Agriculture (USDA) developed the map, basing the zones on the lowest recorded temperatures across North America. Zone 1 is the coldest area and Zone 11 is the warmest.

Plants are classified by the coldest temperature and zone they can endure. For example, plants hardy to Zone 6 survive where winter temperatures drop to –10° F. Those hardy to Zone 8 die long before it's that cold. These plants may grow in colder regions but must be replaced each year. Plants rated for a range of hardiness zones can usually survive winter in the coldest region as well as tolerate the summer heat of the warmest one.

To find your hardiness zone, note the approximate location of your community on the map, then match the color band marking that area to the key.

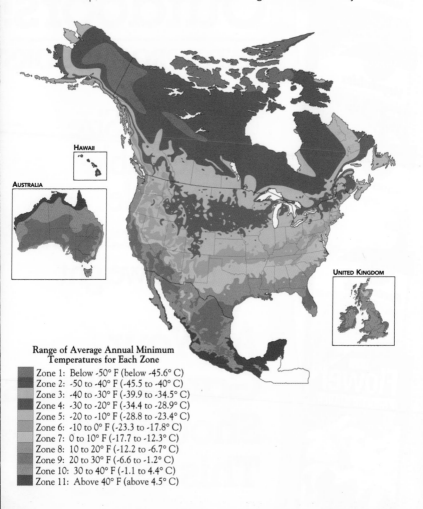

HAWAII

AUSTRALIA

UNITED KINGDOM

Range of Average Annual Minimum Temperatures for Each Zone

Zone 1: Below -50° F (below -45.6° C)
Zone 2: -50 to -40° F (-45.5 to -40° C)
Zone 3: -40 to -30° F (-39.9 to -34.5° C)
Zone 4: -30 to -20° F (-34.4 to -28.9° C)
Zone 5: -20 to -10° F (-28.8 to -23.4° C)
Zone 6: -10 to 0° F (-23.3 to -17.8° C)
Zone 7: 0 to 10° F (-17.7 to -12.3° C)
Zone 8: 10 to 20° F (-12.2 to -6.7° C)
Zone 9: 20 to 30° F (-6.6 to -1.2° C)
Zone 10: 30 to 40° F (-1.1 to 4.4° C)
Zone 11: Above 40° F (above 4.5° C)